Sridhar Balan joined the publishing industry in the early 1980s after a few years teaching at a university, and had long careers with Oxford University Press and Ratna Sagar. He has also been a literary columnist with several Indian newspapers. He is currently a consultant with Ratna Books, an imprint for translations. This is his first book.

OFF THE SHELF

ON BOOKS, BOOK PEOPLE AND PLACES

SRIDHAR BALAN

SPEAKING
TIGER

SPEAKING TIGER BOOKS LLP
125 A, Ground Floor, Shahpur Jat, Near Asiad Village
New Delhi 110049

First published in India by Speaking Tiger 2019

ISBN: 978-93-89231-85-4

10 9 8 7 6 5 4 3 2

Typeset in Sabon Roman by SÜRYA, New Delhi

Printed at Chaman Offset, Delhi

To readers everywhere

To read is to fly; it is to soar to a point of vantage which gives a view over wide terrains of history, human variety, ideas, shared experience and the fruits of many inquiries. A life thus equipped might not be happier—might sometimes be less so, indeed, for to know more can be to feel more—but it is vastly richer.

—A.C. Grayling (from a review of Alberto Manguel's *A History of Reading*)

CONTENTS

FOREWORD

After many years in publishing, meeting writers, editors, booksellers, librarians and readers, Sridhar Balan has written a wonderful book. This is a godsend for those who are in love with the printed word. As a bonus, they also get the history of English publishing in India. Balan has given us an inside account of some major publishing houses on Delhi's Ansari Road and Daryaganj, from the earliest days to recent times. Much of this history unfolded on the typically ill-kept Indian streets coiled around Longmans and Macmillan and Oxford University Press. OUP's aversion to fiction is talked about, though not the new-fangled aversion to poetry. (Someone who climbed up the ladder in the OUP head office on Walton Street must have been bad at poetry, scansion may have appeared as Algebra to him and he must have got it true and proper from a professor at a tutorial. That's how poetry went out.)

The English Novel was introduced to propagate and 'legitimate' Englishness in the colony, we are told. The first three authors introduced into India were G.W.M. Reynolds (1814-79), G.A. Henty (1832-1902) and H. Rider Haggard (1856-1925) of *King Solomon's Mines* fame. You may not have heard of the first two, or all three, but Balan points out that for any great English authors you have read in India, buying their books at Indian prices, you have Reynolds, Henty and Rider Haggard and their publishers to thank.

There are three full essays on OUP India, and the once venerable Press also appears in four or five others. The days OUP progressed under Ravi Dayal showcase one of the great moments in the history of Indian publishing. (Incidentally, there is no mention of Nirupam Chatterjee.)

The book is speckled with nuggets: Borges holding Rudyard Kipling and Robert Louis Stevenson in great regard, going blind in middle age and asking his mother to read for him. The great hullabaloo about Jim Corbett's *Man-Eaters of Kumaon* in New York where tigers made an appearance. Hannah Arendt's pronouncement on Martin Heidegger, whose centenary is being observed (he succumbed to the Nazis): 'You have to separate Martin the man and Heidegger the philosopher.' The incredible story of William Shakespeare's First Folio, which is given an entire chapter. For the uninitiated, it is mind-boggling and must be read.

And there is a fine chapter on the old library of Alexandria. That chapter is a personal favourite, for I am engaged these days in fiction around the Mouseion, as it was called.

Balan has produced a book for connoisseurs.

KEKI N. DARUWALLA

October 2019

PREFACE

PUT THE BLAME ON VODKA

This book is the outcome of a mistake.

Some years ago, a senior publisher decided to do a 'Face-to-Face' with me. In the course of the interview, referring to the columns I had written, he asked me, 'How come you have not written a book as yet?' Over the years, I had indeed written columns in four national dailies at different times and also contributed chapters to books. I paused, reflected for a while, and then answered, 'Because no one has asked me.' This wish was fulfilled when Ravi Singh, the publisher of Speaking Tiger Books, suddenly proposed I write a book about my literary experiences in publishing. We were in the bar of Delhi's India Habitat Centre one balmy evening in the winter of 2017. The vodka Ravi was having must have broken through his defences, as it did through mine, and in a moment of rashness, I agreed. We discussed the matter a little more and I thought no more of it.

I had known Ravi over the years, initially when he was the chief editor and publisher at Penguin. I would run into him intermittently at the Penguin book launches.

We also met at a few seminars and conferences, including one occasion in Chandigarh in 2009, when we were both part of a panel discussion on publishing organized by the Chandigarh Sahitya Akademi. As the session ended, Ravi asked about my return plans to Delhi. I told him I was booked by the evening Shatabdi train. Ravi offered a ride back as he had brought his office car and trusted driver from Delhi. Nothing loth, I cancelled the Shatabdi ticket and ensconced in the rear of Ravi's Ford Ikon, was driven comfortably back to Delhi. At least *I* was comfortable, but perhaps Ravi wasn't. Or maybe the company over a five-hour stretch was a bit much for Ravi, as I did not hear from him for some time. When I finally did, it was through one of his editors who was putting together Penguin India's annual anthology of new writing, *First Proof* (sadly, now defunct). The editor asked if I would like to contribute to the collection. A couple of weeks later, I ran into Ravi at a book launch, and over drinks that evening, told him of an interesting encounter I'd had with the Queen of England at an Indo-British Partnership summit. Slightly incredulous, Ravi asked me to write it up and send it in for *First Proof*. I duly did so, and along with the article, enclosed a scan of a photograph with the Queen. This was the closest I would get to Her Majesty and I thought the world should know. Unfortunately, one of Ravi's editors or production assistants misplaced the photograph and the article was published without it.

Now, some ten years later, during which time he had helped launch Aleph and moved on to set up Speaking Tiger, Ravi was offering me a chance to write a whole book! Perhaps he was conscious of having ruined my chances of immortality by losing that photo with the English Queen. This offer was an act of atonement. Decent fellow, I thought, also poor fellow, chuckling to myself. And, as I've said, I thought no more of it.

With the Queen!

In January 2018, I called Ravi. My wife was away travelling, I was alone. 'Why don't we do a D&D at home this evening?' I asked Ravi. For the uninitiated, D&D refers to 'dosas and drinks'. Ravi happily agreed and came over and in his hands was a publishing contract! I had a look and found that the details more or less corresponded to what we had discussed that evening in the IHC bar. Once the contract was before us on the table, Ravi was all business-like. He said I would have to initial every page and sign at the end on two copies and he would do likewise. One copy was for him and the other for me. He then entered my name by hand, and looking around the house, asked, 'Address?' I suddenly realized we couldn't put the address we were living in at the time as that was only temporary till we moved back to our own place in Hauz Khas which was being refurbished. Ravi looked doubtful when I told him this but readily put down a future address when I swore that I wasn't lying. Now came the tricky part, the deadline for the manuscript. I tentatively ventured, 'In a year?' and looked around hopefully for the drinks to arrive. 'Oh no,' said Ravi. 'We will put down August 2018,' and proceeded to do so. 'We can always extend the date,' he said cheerfully, looking at my crestfallen face.

He then put down the length. 'Shall we say 40,000 words or 30,000?' he asked, then added, 'Whatever you're comfortable with.' I was, by now, most uncomfortable. 'Whatever,' I said weakly. Ravi wrote down 'App. 35,000 words,' settled back in the sofa and said, 'Now we can have a drink.'

My wife duly returned and in an unguarded moment happened to read the contract. Her eyes travelled down to the publishing deadline and to the length. She then read all the punitive clauses that publishers usually put in case the manuscript is not delivered on time, and the bit which said that any dispute between publisher and author would have to be settled in a court within the jurisdiction of Delhi. 'You had better start writing,' she said.

I knew there was no way I could complete the

manuscript by August 2018. At Ratna Sagar, where I am a consultant, we had just launched a new imprint, Ratna Books, exclusively for translations from different Indian languages into English, and my help would be needed to get it off the ground. There would be some travel, too. Months passed. By now, the word had gone around the family that I was writing a book. 'How's the book coming along?' asked sister and brother-in-law in unison whenever they called long-distance from Toronto. 'Has he started writing every day?' asked sister-in-law from Bengaluru. I was spared any inquiry from my other sister, who was far too busy shunting between Delhi and Kamshet with side-trips to Mumbai, Pune, Chennai, Kolkata and Goa to bother about my book. Moreover, she had published her own book a couple of years ago and knew exactly what it involved. She probably felt sorry for me.

'Give me something, at least,' said the wife one day, 'so that I may answer all queries honestly.'

So now I knew I had to do *something* and fully sympathized with Jim Corbett's predicament. Corbett was once relating some of his adventures in the jungles of north India to friends at a government function, when the divisional commissioner's wife at the adjoining table overheard him. Later, she came over and asked Corbett whether he had ever thought of writing up his experiences. Corbett confessed he hadn't. At this point, the lady expressed great surprise and made Corbett feel rather guilty that he had not done so. In order to not meet the lady again, Corbett began avoiding government functions altogether. Till an occasion came where the governor himself would be present and Corbett's presence was required. Knowing that he would meet the commissioner's wife again and not wishing to hurt the lady's feelings, Corbett resolved to do something. He took out his typewriter, put a sheet of paper in, and typed, 'JUNGLE STORIES—Chapter One'. Sure enough, at the reception the lady came around and asked Corbett whether he had done anything at all. Corbett replied truthfully, 'Lady, I have made a start!'

Typewriters being obsolete, I took out my laptop and typed out 'In the Beginning'.

'What are you doing?' asked the wife.

'Being a bit like Corbett,' I said.

Quite unimpressed, she said, 'I want to see something on paper,' adding, 'you always call Ravi when I am not here. I want to meet him too.'

'But I don't,' I said and retreated to my den.

But August was looming large and now my wife had changed her query to ask: 'Where's the book?' to which I replied, 'But Ravi had assured me the time can be extended...' She gave me a look, and then she reminded me that she hadn't been introduced to my publisher yet. Would I ever?

I had to finally call Ravi for yet another D&D at home. By this time, I had written up three chapters. When my wife said we would have to show Ravi something, I emailed the three chapters to her. She took printouts. Ravi strode in and asked, 'Where's the book?' I countered by asking whether he would like a vodka-tonic. 'Never mind the vodka, where's the book?' he asked again, peaceably but firmly. He meant business. 'You said I could take my time,' I reminded him. This time *he* gave me a look. So I gave him the three chapters.

Ravi seemed to like—or at least not dislike—what little he quickly read. 'Where's the vodka?' he asked, suddenly relaxing.

I then broached the issue of extending the deadline. Ravi changed the time limit very generously to January 2019. He explained to my slightly surprised wife that most authors never delivered manuscripts within the first time stipulation.

I got down to serious work now. Radhika—that's my wife—was not too happy that Ravi was a 'hands-off' publisher who allowed authors to mostly work at their own pace. 'I wish he would keep pushing you now and again,' she said, reminding me that I worked better with deadlines. She was also worried that my old laptop might develop a glitch or the disk may crash. As a precaution, she asked me to email each chapter to her as soon as it was finished, ostensibly to ensure it was saved in her laptop just in case mine crashed, but more I suspect to keep tabs on my progress.

So, I wrote and wrote, thinking wistfully of Alberto Manguel who in his *A History of Reading* wrote the last page first! I should never have accepted Ravi's guilt-driven offer. 'I made a mistake,' I wanted to tell my wife. 'Writing a book is torture. And he'll probably ask me to revise it.' But she had no sympathy.

At last it was done, and we were able to call Ravi

home for yet another D&D and show him the complete manuscript. It was duly handed over, and now it was my turn. I rang up Ravi the next day and asked, 'Where's the book?'

*

And now, for the benefit of everyone, here's the Book!

Before a publisher puts out a book into the market, I feel that much like Gandhi, the image of the poor reader must flash before him. He would need to ask: 'Will this book benefit the reader?' Anthony Trollope, whose works are now considered classics, once stated, 'Of all the merits a book possesses, its chief merit should be that it be readable.' If you, dear reader, flip through these pages and decide that the book does not quite pass Trollope's test, nothing more needs to be said. If, on the other hand, you are indeed tempted to go further, I would urge you to dip into the book at leisure and read any chapter you fancy. Each of the chapters has a story to tell and some chapters subsume other stories within themselves. Of some you may be aware and some may be new. I would be happy to have your feedback.

SRIDHAR BALAN

New Delhi

IN THE BEGINNING...

It was a remark by Mark Tully, for many years the voice of the BBC in India and now a reputed writer on the country, that set me thinking about the history of English books in the Subcontinent. The occasion was the launch of *For Pepper and Christ*, a novel by the eminent poet Keki Daruwalla, based on the voyages of Vasco da Gama. Mark was the chief guest, and while unwrapping the book, he said, 'It reads like a swashbuckling novel of adventure by Henty, whose books I read during my schooldays in England.' Mark also made a rather good attempt at depicting a duel with swords, so typical of the Henty novels, to illustrate his remark. At the reception which followed the launch, I went up to Mark and Keki and said that Mark's reference to Henty, while so apt, was perhaps properly understood by just the three of us in the year 2009. And indeed, quite a few young and not-so-young attendees of the launch function came up to Mark wanting to know who this Henty fellow was!

G.A. Henty was among the first three authors to be promoted by English publishing firms in India, which led to the consolidation of a market for English books in this part of the world—the 'fun and games' aspect of the Empire, if you will.

In 1835, Thomas Babington Macaulay in his famous 'Minute on Education' advocated English as the medium of instruction in schools and colleges all over India. He wished to create a subaltern class, 'a class of persons, Indian in blood and colour but English in taste, in opinions, in morals and in intellect'. While Macaulay's intention was to better consolidate British rule in the Subcontinent—and he never actually believed that Indians could match the English in 'opinions, morals' or 'intellect'—educating Indians in English was to have far-reaching consequences. Introducing Indians to the work of English novelists was an ideal way of fulfilling Macaulay's dream. As Priya Joshi in her book *In Another Country: Colonialism, Culture and the English Novel in India* notes, '...the British novel was introduced in India in the nineteenth century as a means of propagating and legitimating Englishness in the colony.' While Joshi goes on to study the impact of the English novel in the Subcontinent—'the consumption patterns of the English novel among Indian readers from 1835-1900'—it is worth considering how Macaulay's resolution also helped to grow and consolidate the *market* for English books in these parts.

It was a process that had been started in the first half of the nineteenth century by visiting journeymen, the original 'carpetbaggers' representing English publishing firms, who sold English books to both the official and non-official British citizens working in support services and other professions, and also to the very small number of Indians, probably a few hundred, who had English at the time. But now, with Macaulay's Minute making English the medium of instruction in India, the demand for English books was poised to grow dramatically. Based on the reports of the travelling journeymen, two significant developments took place. One was the establishment of the 'Colonial Library' series, initially begun by John Murray's Home and Colonial Library in 1843 and then joined by other publishers, notably Macmillan some forty years later. The second development was the physical presence of English publishing firms in India, making a transformation from travelling representatives. A Longman Green sales depot was set up in 1895, followed soon after by the Macmillan Company of India. Barely a decade later, Oxford University Press (OUP) established an office in Bombay in 1912.

The first three English authors promoted in India were G.W.M. Reynolds (1814-79), G.A. Henty (1832-1902) and H. Rider Haggard (1856-1925). All three were to gain immense popularity here and, in fact, continued to remain popular long after they had ceased to be actually read.

Reynolds was the author of over fifty books, the most notable among them being *The Mysteries of London* and *Mysteries of the Court of London*. His books had all the ingredients of melodrama to keep the reader hooked. Children changed at birth, fortunes and inheritances fell into the wrong hands, ruthless villains struck at the innocent, and brave protagonists subjected to relentless trials finally emerged victorious in the end—the villains were defeated and all was well with the world. Initially,

Reynolds's books were serialized in popular weeklies and this greatly helped to establish a dedicated readership. Reynolds in his heyday achieved a fame greater than any other contemporary author, including Dickens, but is virtually unknown to anyone other than the specialist researcher today. Interestingly, even as Reynolds was enjoying great success in British India, interest in him was already declining in Europe; he wasn't even half as popular in his home country. Priya Joshi writes of an encounter in the 1920s between Mulk Raj Anand, then an aspiring writer, and Virginia Woolf. Hoping to impress Woolf, Anand told her that he had read all of G.W.M. Reynolds's works and hoped that the famed author's long sentences had not influenced his own writing. After the meeting, a perplexed Woolf is said to have asked her husband Leonard Woolf, 'But who on *earth* is G.W.M. Reynolds?'

George Alfred Henty was even more prolific than Reynolds. He wrote some 120 books, mostly history adventure stories for younger people. As a child, he was sick for prolonged periods of time, and frequently confined to his bed for weeks, he became a voracious reader. He was later to say that his ability to write stories also grew out of the stories he listened to while in hospital and at home. Commissioned in the army during the Crimean War, Henty vividly described the conditions he saw at the front in his letters home. His father, impressed with the quality of his letters, sent them to newspapers which published them. Henty soon resigned his army commission to become a war correspondent and covered the action in the Franco-Prussian War, the Ashanti War and the British Expedition to Abyssinia. He also travelled to Russia, Palestine and India and witnessed the historic opening of the Suez Canal. These travels fuelled his imagination, and many thrilling adventures—real and wished for—found their way into his novels. Among his popular books were *Cat of Bubastes: A Tale of Ancient Egypt*; *In Freedom's Cause: A Story of Bruce and Wallace*; *A Knight of the White Cross: A Tale of the Siege of Rhodes* and *By Conduct and Courage: A Story of Nelson's Days*. He also wrote a number of books set in India: *With Clive in India, Or, The Beginnings of an Empire*; *At the Point of the Bayonet: A Tale of the Mahratta War* and *The Tiger of Mysore: A Story of the War with Tippoo Saib*. These tales

of adventure and 'derring do' were staple fare for school children in England and in India too; though there was a decent gap between Mark Tully's school days and mine, we had both read and enjoyed Henty's books immensely. I still remember discussing Henty's description of the war between Carthage and Rome in school, and only recently, I found myself recalling in a casual conversation the name of the Carthaginian general Hannibal—over half a century after I had read Henty's *The Young Carthaginian: A Story of the Times of Hannibal*!

Henry Rider Haggard (1856-1925) was easily the best known among the three early authors promoted by the Colonial Library in India. Unsuccessful in his quest for a career in the army, Rider Haggard was sent by his father in 1875 for service in the governor's office in the province of Natal in South Africa and later in the Boer Republic of the Transvaal, which was later annexed by the British. His adventure stories were set in South Africa, and notable among them are the ever-popular *King Solomon's Mines* (credited with having started the whole 'lost world' genre of fiction), *She* and *Allan Quatermain*. He also produced sequels, like *Ayesha: The Return of She; Ancient Allan*; *Allan's Wife* and *Hunter Quatermain's Story*. As both She and Quatermain became his most popular characters, Rider Haggard also brought them together in the novel *She and Allan*. *King Solomon's Mines* remains Rider Haggard's best-known work and is widely read to this day. With remarkable foresight, Rider Haggard accepted 10 per cent royalty for this novel from his publisher over an outright flat fee of 100 pounds for transfer of copyright. The book became an instant bestseller when it was published—in 1885—and has sold many millions of copies since.

In India too Rider Haggard's books sold huge numbers, especially after they received a boost when they became required reading in schools. In the 1960s I was studying in a residential school in the Nilgiri Hills, and I vividly recall that during my holidays I would help my cousins plow through *King Solomon's Mines* which had been prescribed for non-detailed reading at their day school in Coimbatore!

The 'colonial library' was a sort of omnibus term to underscore the efforts of English publishers to popularize English books in India and to develop a market for them. To this end, books meant for the colonial library were exclusively printed for India and priced to suit the Indian market conditions. At the peak of the project, about nine publishers ran colonial library editions—Bentley, Bell, Murray, Heinemann, Cassells, Longman, Kegan Paul, Frederick Warne and Macmillan. The efforts of John Murray, Kegan Paul and Macmillan were the most prominent.

Murray began its Colonial and Home Library series in 1843. Though the titles were meant for sale in Britain's overseas colonies, the major consuming market was India. While in part Murray depended on the tour reports of the travelling salesmen, it also responded to feedback from prominent travel writers like Emma Roberts and John Kaye, who said good literature was hard to come by in India. Through its Colonial and Home Library, from 1843 till it wound up in 1849, Murray produced a range of fiction, poetry, travel writing, history, memoirs and biographies for its readers in India. Murray's trail-blazing effort proved decisively that there was a market for English books in the Subcontinent.

Though books continued to be made available in India through the efforts of other publishers and their representatives after Murray's series wound up, it wasn't until 1886-87 that the next major initiatives were undertaken by the bigger English publishers. A notable initiative came from Kegan Paul, which promoted about 107 titles through its Indian and Colonial Library Series in just two years, 1887-89. (However, due to differences within the firm, it does not appear to have made the range of its formidable fiction list available in India.)

But the most significant, long-term enterprise in the colonial library series has to be that of Macmillan's. This famous firm, which began its Colonial Library in 1886, made available about 193 titles in India. Moreover, it took great care over its production standards in spite of the differential pricing. All the titles in its Colonial Library Series had a distinct and attractive look. In most cases, books for this series appeared simultaneously with the editions published for England; in some cases, even earlier. Strengthened by its own office in India and confident that the Colonial Library would add considerably to its revenues, Macmillan engaged one of the most expensive printers of the time, R&R Clark of Edinburgh, to print its titles for India.

Due to the colonial library project, hundreds of

prominent authors—mainly English, but also some from the rest of Europe in English translation—provided literary and intellectual nourishment to an ever-growing tribe of Indian readers then, as they do now. To name just a few: Jane Austen, Wilkie Collins, Hugh Conway, Marie Corelli, Daniel Defoe, Charles Dickens, Lewis Carroll, Arthur Conan Doyle, Alexandre Dumas, George Eliot, Henry Fielding, H. Rider Haggard, G. A. Henty, Thomas Hardy, Anthony Hope, Victor Hugo, Charles Kingsley, Rudyard Kipling, Capt. Frederick Marryat, George Meredith, G.W. Reynolds, Sir Walter Scott, R.L. Stevenson, Meadows Taylor, W.M. Thackeray, Leo Tolstoy, Anthony Trollope, Mark Twain, Emile Zola and Henry James.

These were riches indeed. Macaulay may have a lot to answer for. But it cannot be denied that his mission also ended up bringing some great literature to millions of Indian readers, helping them discover and engage with whole new worlds. And of course, many 'subalterns' went on to use English to subvert Macaulay's colonizing mission in ways he hadn't imagined.

As always, history challenges us by refusing to be straightforward.

READING THE BOOK—READING THE WORLD

The route to choosing a career in publishing may vary, and for many, it may not have been a conscious career choice at all. Indeed, till recently many people joined the Indian publishing industry having only a very rudimentary idea of what they were getting into, with the sole exception of those who joined the family profession of publishing or bookselling. So, it is remarkable that in spite of the uncertainties, people stayed on in the profession. I belong to a publishing generation characterized by longevity. I never cease to tell the participants in the introductory course on publishing conducted by the National Book Trust (NBT), of which I have been on the faculty since its inception, to ask their guest faculty how many years they have worked in the profession. They would be surprised at the years of experience many of the faculty have—in some cases far longer than the students have been on the planet!

The qualifications for a job in publishing may vary but none of them were technical back in my day, unless you acquired a diploma in printing technology and wanted to work in the production department. It was much later that qualified graphic designers would join in the design department or bright young MBAs in marketing. For one, the salaries in publishing were hardly competitive and this is true the world over. My former boss and mentor at Oxford University press (OUP), Ravi Dayal, mentioned to me in the year that I was recruited—1985—that it was his intention to keep salaries in publishing roughly apace with those paid to academic faculties in universities. Having recently taught at a central university, I told him there was already a gap between the respective salaries; publishing paid much less. In the intervening years, with revisions of the pay grades by the University Grants Commission (UGC) and successive pay commissions, the gap has only grown.

Why then would one want to join a profession that was relatively underpaid? A senior colleague, Santosh Mookerjee, Ravi's deputy in OUP for many years, described publishing as a 'gentleman's profession', as indeed had many men before him. The emphasis being on the word 'gentleman'! Not bad, I thought later, for someone who tried to sell me the job in OUP, after the initial interview by Ravi, on the basis of the subsidized lunch that was served to the staff! Another senior in the profession, N.R. Subramanian, who was the executive director of Tata McGraw Hill, once told me 'publishers [were] incorrigible optimists' who looked for a silver lining after the dark clouds had dissipated. Another colleague, Rukun Advani, now a distinguished academic publisher in his own right, said 'a good editor' (or even a publisher) had to be 'a failed academic', recalling perhaps the time he had taught at St. Stephen's College in Delhi before going off to Cambridge on an Inlaks fellowship.

All these qualities have to do more with temperament and a state of mind than anything else. (And they have nothing at all to do with being a 'gentleman'; gentlewomen in publishing have been proving this for decades, though until about a decade ago hardly any of them were celebrated or even noticed.) I joined publishing via academics and perhaps might qualify for Rukun's definition of a 'failed academic'. I had two teaching stints, one at the Jawaharlal Nehru University (JNU), Delhi on an 'ad hoc' basis and the other as a member of the faculty at the North Eastern Hill University (NEHU), Shillong. I enjoyed teaching, but having made the decision to come back to Delhi from Shillong, I chose publishing after an initial stint at the Centre for Policy Research. I worked for two years with Macmillan India before being interviewed successfully by Ravi Dayal for a job in OUP in 1985. I emphasize 'successfully' because the rejections from Ravi's interviews were almost as numerous as his rejections of manuscripts from hopeful authors. In the course of a long and meandering interview, of almost an hour, Ravi wanted to establish two things: my level and standard of English, and whether I liked books and reading and if I did, the authors I had read. No wonder the interview took an hour, my friends will say! But Ravi pronounced himself satisfied on both counts and I got the job.

This actually brings me to the one primary qualification that makes one eminently suitable for a job in publishing, and this is, to quote hundreds who have said it before me, 'a love for books and a passion for reading'. Though born in Odisha, I spent my formative years in what was still Calcutta and studied up to Class 5 in a school there. The advantage of studying in an Anglo-Indian school in those years was that it laid a foundation for strong skills in English and also exposed you to books and literature. I developed a good command of English and books kindled a life-long interest in the written—and printed—word. In fact, I managed to top the class in the annual Class 4 examinations and got the prize for general proficiency! Things looked rosy indeed till I entered Class 5 and Hindi kicked in. Schools in Calcutta had a high standard in Hindi which was a compulsory second language. I could now barely manage pass marks and quite often, failed. But the passion for books and reading continued. We had the elements of a small library at home with our own collections, mostly books that I and my sisters had won as prizes in school. I also belonged to a generation which received books as gifts at birthday parties and I remember being presented with a copy of Louisa Alcott's *Good Wives* by a girl who lived in the neighbourhood. The poor girl had perhaps not chosen the book herself but I was ribbed on the gift by elder cousins in the family asking me what her intentions were. I remember for some time I read Alcott surreptitiously, not wanting to be teased further.

Our library at home was greatly embellished with the multi-volume *Book of Knowledge*, the *Reader's Digest* Encyclopaedic Dictionaries and the Gem's Classics. The introduction of a range of classics in the family was the beginning of another tradition, that of 'story reading'. My father had left his home in Kerala, had seen service in Burnpur and Odisha, before moving to Calcutta, and led a busy life at the office. Conscious perhaps that he had missed out on opportunities to read and have books as a part of his life, and being a little too busy to take up reading now (he was to do so many years later), he got my elder sister Jaya to read for him. Jaya was an early fan of the Bronte sisters. So *Jane Eyre* and *Wuthering Heights* were read with verve and passion. Jaya was a wonderful reader and my father was riveted. I used to listen in, while passing, but was too young to be a formal part of these sessions. Even when the reading sessions were interrupted when he went on tour, father would get Jaya to resume where she had left off, on his return. These slightly interrupted sessions were to stand my father in good stead later on, when he would ask my mother to read the stories from the Tamil periodicals she subscribed to—*Ananda Vikatan*, *Kalki* and *Kumudam*. Many of these stories were serialized and my father had to wait for the reading session to resume only after the next issue arrived.

My mother used to subscribe to these Tamil periodicals in Calcutta. They were published in Chennai, then Madras, and there was a slight time lag before they were available with the local vendor. Sometimes, I had to check with the vendor the reason for the delay. Later, my mother got them through mail from Chennai. These periodicals were very popular with the reading public and their circulation was in the lakhs. They were priced reasonably as they were printed on newsprint, and there would be a furore if there was even a slight increase in their published price. The noted Tamil writer Krishnamurthy had founded the periodical *Kalki* and he took this as his pen name while writing his stories. My mother used to have successive copies of *Kalki* bound and ship them to my grandmother in Thrissur, Kerala. My paternal grandmother, widowed at an early stage, had adopted the path of spiritualism and apart from her pujas, reading 'Kalki' was her one passion. Krishnamurthy, unfortunately, died at a young age and I remember something my mother told me at the time. When Krishnamurthy died, it was a shock for his many fans and his peers in Tamil literary circles. My mother said that grandmother had written to her remarking in Tamil on Kalki's death: 'In Krishnamurthy's passing, I feel as if a close member of the family has passed away.' I was to reflect on this and marvel at Kalki's craft, that he could touch a reader so deeply.

Coming back to my early schooling, perhaps it was concern about my lack of prowess in Hindi, or perhaps that I should acquire some independent skills, that led to my being packed off, in the early 1960s, to a boarding school in faraway Ooty in the salubrious Nilgiri Hills of south India. I am not too sure as to what skills I picked up at the Laidlaw Memorial High School of St. George's in Ketti, Nilgiris, but my passion for books and reading continued in the six years that I was there. The school kept us busy during the working week, but in spite of a hectic games and sports schedule, I devoured the library. The hills were particularly conducive to reading and the woods were the ideal setting in which to lose oneself in the magic of books, particularly as there was no television in those years to distract us. I eventually passed out of school with a first class and proudly sported a distinction in Hindi! I also proudly treasured the books I received as prizes for my performance in Hindi each year, with the last ones being Dumas's *The Three Musketeers* and *The Count of Monte Cristo* (yes, English translations of French classics as reward for excelling in Hindi—plain absurd, some might say, but to me, wonderfully cosmopolitan). Many years later, while in Goa, I was to see the statue dedicated to Abbe Faria, the father of hypnotism, and learn that Dumas had based his character of the Abbe in the prison on the Chateau d'If on Faria, whom he had met in France.

I was to receive a school leaving certificate from the principal who described me as 'a voracious reader', so my 'devouring of books' was not quite out of character! But the real reward was when I used to visit relatives in Coimbatore during the occasional month-end break and my cousins there would ask me to summarize the story of Rider Haggard's *King Solomon's Mines.* It had been prescribed as a 'non-detailed' text in their school and they, preparing eventually for a career in accountancy and engineering, just could not be bothered to read it. For my part, I wondered why it was not prescribed as a 'detailed' text. Besides Rider Haggard's works, I had been exposed to three Shakespeare texts in school, *The Merchant of Venice*, *Julius Caesar* and *Richard II.* We used the Arden edition of Shakespeare and its critical apparatus in the form of a long introduction was formidable. Our drama texts also included Galsworthy's *Strife*. 'The Romance of Reading' course books in the lower classes had of course already exposed us to many other gems of English literature.

Those were the days of long winter breaks. Our school closed for two months in winter and these were spent in Calcutta catching up on movies and reading. I soon joined the Oxford Lending Library at the rear of the Oxford Book and Stationery shop on Calcutta's fabled Park Street. They had a good number of books in hardback with outer polythene covers. My reading matured as I did, and when I joined college in Calcutta, it was great to get book coupons as prizes for doing well in individual subjects. The college had a tie-up with Allied Publishers. The only pity was that the combined prices of the books we wanted always exceeded the value of the book coupon and we had to dig into our pocket money to make up the difference. One of my more prized book gifts was from my history teacher in college, Father Schepers—Stefan Zweig's memoir, *The World of Yesterday*, which I still have. They were clearing the college library of old books and the good Father had thought that this was a book I should have. And I have indeed cherished it ever since, going back to it every few years to savour the glorious portrait of Vienna in the dying days of the Austro-Hungarian empire—enlightened and culturally and intellectually vibrant. The last brilliance before the flame went out. The good Father Schepers taught European history with verve, zest and drama and had been walking in Antwerp when the Armistice to mark the end of World War I was signed. We would not forget his reading from Emil Ludwig's biography of Napoleon and Voltaire's quote on the Holy Roman empire, that it was neither holy, nor Roman and not even an empire!

Both my sisters attended one of the finest schools in Calcutta for English language teaching, the Modern High School for Girls, and they did well in debates and elocution too. My younger sister Lalita also added some prowess in quiz competitions to her skills and once appeared along with the historian and now biographer Ram Guha in the India Quiz programme. Ram must have wondered later that with such a bright sibling, how had I turned out as I did! In addition to her prize books, Lalita won some books from the German Radio broadcaster Deutsche Welle. Among the books were *The Lenz Papers* by Stefan Heym and *Ricefield-Battlefield*, a history of the Vietnam war by Kurt Stern. *The Lenz Papers* by Heym is fascinating in the best traditions of the historical novel. It speaks of a time of great ferment in Germany, or more properly speaking, Prussia, and the failed 1848 revolution in the Grand Duchy of Baden. Andreas Lenz, poet, philosopher and soldier, is the main protagonist and both Marx and Engels appear in the book with a lecture by Engels on the role of the peasant in history. The book was published in 1968 by Seven Seas publishers in Berlin, in what was still the German Democratic Republic. This book made quite an impression on me, and years later I wrote about it in my column in *The Hindu*.

*

All this reading prepared me for the profession that was to shape my life. After years of reading the work of great scholars, I found myself working with their kind in India. My long years in publishing helped me forge great friendships with some fine academics who were authors at OUP. At a request from the India Habitat Centre in the early 2000s, I was able to organize a series of lectures there. Andre Beteille kicked this off with a fine lecture on M.N. Srinivas, followed by T.N (or Loki) Madan on religion in India, Dipankar Gupta on social stratification and Upen Baxi on human rights.

In 2005, I joined the publishers Ratna Sagar with possibly the shortest appointment letter in history. The letter, more like an invitation, stated that I was to come in as a senior consultant to help Ratna Sagar grow. It was signed by the founder, Dhanesh Jain, who started the company in 1982 to bring the best of content and design to school books. My brief was to help organize academic oriented programmes based on the content of Ratna Sagar's books for school teachers, especially in the humanities and English. English Language Teaching (ELT) is among the most prestigious subjects taught in schools all over India. English being the dominant global language that it is, most people believe a sound foundation in this language will help in any career objective. Parents depended on schools to provide this foundation and schools decided that they would ensure they had the best books in English. But for an indigenous publisher like Ratna Sagar, it was not easy to gain business in ELT, since the market was dominated by the more established international publishers.

Soon after I joined, I realized that if we were to gain some market share in English, we had to change our image of being a publisher primarily of science textbooks. We needed to be perceived by schools as an innovative ELT publisher. Fortunately for us, around the same time, the Central Board of Secondary Education (CBSE) fraternity began to adopt a 'communicative' approach to the teaching of English, where the students are perceived as 'active participants' in the learning process. This helped us a great deal as our books were already patterned on this method. Gradually, our business in English began to rise. During my interactions with school principals, I came across a common refrain—our children are fast losing interest in reading, they would say; could something be done to rekindle their interest in books and develop reading as a habit? Regardless of what books might look like in the future, and whether reading from print might become passé and obsolete, I resolved that if reading itself was to be kept alive, we needed to motivate our children. I therefore structured a programme on reading called 'Reading the Book—Reading the World', but my audience was the teaching community, many of whom were parents too. I hoped to use them as catalysts to inspire and motivate their students and children to read.

In the programme, I told the teachers if reading as a habit was to be formed and was to endure in later life, it needed to begin first at home. I urged them to revive the near extinct oral story-telling culture at home, perhaps continuing a tradition where as children they may have heard stories from their own grandparents or parents.

After some time, I told them, they could switch to 'reading' stories. They would need to do this as children would like to hear a new story every day, and books had an almost endless collection of stories. It was important to establish a relationship between the child and the book. I told them of my own experience—of hearing stories, indeed, entire books, read out by my sister to my father, and how much I had benefitted from it.

In addition to reading, I urged the teachers to 'act' out their stories. If action followed words, the children would listen entranced. Even somewhat shy teachers could lose their inhibitions and afford to be a little bold in the privacy of their homes. In the school, they could look at the library as a valuable resource and 'decorate' the walls and the notice-board with additional information on the authors whose books they stocked in the library. And I urged the teachers to allow free access to the books in the library. They should not worry overmuch about damage to the books. If this did happen inadvertently, a teacher could simply give paper, scissors and glue to the child and ask her or him to 'repair' the damage. A child who had repaired a book was not likely to damage it again.

Invariably, I would conclude the programme on reading with a short story that I would read out to the teachers myself. Often humorous, the specially selected story was intended to test their imagination. My aim was to show them that a good story impacted our mind immediately, and continued to do so in different ways over time. As we read or hear a story, we unconsciously visualize the descriptions and episodes. It is this visual aspect that enriches the reading experience, our imagination and indeed our lives. I often quoted Ruskin Bond to the teachers: 'Reading these stories, you will come across new words and new worlds too. For in his or her imagination, a great writer can take you almost anywhere—across the seas, or into the forests, or up into the starry sky. And through the magic of the writers' words, you can share their thoughts, feelings, experiences. A love of reading goes hand in hand with a love of life.'

A few of the teachers did query me about finding the time to read. I told them if we are serious about reading, we need to factor in the necessary time as we would do for all the other activities that we consider essential—while travelling or during weekends, for instance. There really is no excuse not to.

But if I have to be honest, I must admit that if we wish to truly enjoy the reading experience, to be enriched by it, brief periods over weekends or stolen moments on flights or the metro are no good. Sustained reading simply cannot be done just anywhere. We need an ambience that is peaceful and without disturbance. Above all, we need to be seated comfortably. We must find and cherish our own favourite chair in which to sit and read. Comfort and quiet are non-negotiable. Turning to Alberto Manguel again, in his book *A History of Reading*, he gives us the illustration of a chair used by reading libraries in England in the eighteenth century. The illustration Manguel reproduces and describes is from 1720. The chair had leather upholstery, comfortable armrests, and a wooden rest very handy for reading heavy books. The wooden rest was designed to fit at the back of the chair, so the reader had to sit astride, turning his or her back to the audience, symbolic, perhaps, of a retreat into a private world of reading.

BOOKS ARE MEMORIES ON SHELVES

During the programmes that I help conduct to enhance reading skills in schools, I try to gauge the teachers' own relationship to books. While home may be a modest apartment, is there a defined place for books and, equally important, a place for children's books as well? A few hands do go up but they are only a few. We do not seem to have a place for books in our homes and yet we want our children to read. Is it possible that our teachers as parents are very tech savvy and the printed book has been replaced with the Kindle and other e-readers? No, the e-readers are absent too. We are busy filling our homes with curios and various objets d'art, and quite happy to show off our latest acquisitions to visitors. Even where we devote some space to books, the books somehow seem to be survivors of a relentless war to obliterate them. I ask my audience to ponder over the fact that when we shift homes or are intent on 'decluttering', books usually become the first casualty. They are expendable, do not protest and no one seems to care or even miss them. Unless you happen to be a book lover and an avid reader; then it hurts.

Sometimes, the mere presence of books on the

shelves can calm and reassure us. I often give the example of the 9/11 attacks on New York City. After the first plane had crashed into one of the twin towers of the World Trade Center, the authorities were informed by intelligence that a second plane was bound for the other tower. In the few precious minutes that were left, they tried to evacuate as many people as they could to safety. Residents were quickly taken down to the basement and through the silent subway tunnels. Emerging on to the street a few blocks away, they took shelter in a Borders Bookstore that had been hurriedly opened for them. While nothing could compensate for their fear and trauma, it is recorded that the sight of books neatly stacked on shelves did go some way to calm their nerves and bring some element of sanity amidst the chaos and horror.

I am, again, reminded of Ruskin Bond—his own deep, intimate and intrinsic relationship with books.

We Who Love Books

Some books I'll never give away,
Though old and worn, their binding torn,
Upon my shelves they'll always stay,
Alive, still read, still fresh, each dawn,
Their magic moments never gone.

Familiar friends, these timeless tales,
Have been with me since I was ten,
And as I turn their pages once again,
I feel and love their old refrain.

Great verse, great thoughts
Still stand the test
Of time that's passing by so fast...

These good companions never fail
To give me joy, to nourish me.
We who love books will always be
The lucky ones, our minds set free.

Wonderful thoughts by Ruskin that give succour to many a book lover. And sometimes, the book lover has to fight to retain a place for books. The noted evangelist and crusader for books and reading, Alberto Manguel, Argentinian by birth, Canadian by nationality and French by domicile, shifted residence from Toronto to the Loire district in France simply to have enough space to house all his books. He found a fifteenth-century French chateau adequate for him and his partner, but was more attracted to the barn that came with it. Used in bygone years to house horses, the barn, Manguel felt, if properly refurbished could just about fit his modest collection of 30,000 books. But till this could be done, he had to store all his beloved books in cases. Lost without the familiar sight of his books on shelves, Manguel began to pull out a book or two every day from the cases and tried to remember where he had got them. Gazing at them, he remembered the scribbled note on the flyleaf, a bookmark, and an occasional note marking a page, the reason for it now forgotten. 'My memory is less interested in me than in my books,' he wrote, 'and I find it easier to remember the story read once, than the young man who read it.'

The library was finally completed and Manguel was able to display almost all his books, though quite a few found their way into the main house. Manguel and his partner had a blissful time for fifteen years till the French raised problems about his prolonged stay without a certificate of domicile. And he had to pack again. 'Packing,' he noted, 'is an exercise in oblivion. It is like playing a film backwards, consigning visible narratives and methodological reality to the regions of the distant and unseen, a voluntary forgetting.' I could well sympathize with Manguel's plight as my own far more modest library went through its own two phases of packing, one when we had to leave our home as it was being redesigned and again when we moved back after a year. Some may wonder why I bothered to unpack the books in the temporary accommodation. But how could I exist without books for a whole year? Moreover, I needed the books for my own writing references and for my programmes on reading. My friend Usha, the architect-writer from Bengaluru, faced a similar plight when she moved from Kolkata to Bengaluru to her new home. The only problem was that the home was not ready and she had to stay for a little more than a year in an apartment they had invested in. But Usha could not do without her books and even here, she displayed them, but alas, space permitted only a fraction of her collection. She invited us to her new home, since completed, recently—my wife, to show her the architecture and design, and me, I suspect, to show me the entire collection of books proudly stacked from floor to ceiling.

Ruskin's poem indicates that his book collection began at the age of ten. Manguel received his first book as a gift, H.G. Wells's *The Island of Dr Moreau*, on his tenth birthday. I am not sure if I can remember all the books I received on my tenth birthday and the others that followed while I was in school—*Good Wives* by Louisa M. Alcott was one of them, and there were other classics too, like Jules Verne's *Twenty-thousand Leagues Under the Sea* and Dumas's *The Three Musketeers*. In those early days, the books at home were mainly reference volumes and classic literature. My father would stock the shelves with the *Book of Knowledge*, the multi-volume reference series that was for some reason preferred over the better-known *Encyclopaedia Britannica*. I used to wonder at this and later realized that the distributor had employed some aggressive salespersons who would target corporate offices for orders. In spite of being busy, my father found time to meet these people as purveyors of books were put on a higher pedestal than sellers of other products. There must have been some group discount offers, for we found the same books at the homes of my father's colleague too. So the *Gem's Classics* and the *Reader's Digest Encyclopedic Dictionaries* too found their way to our shelves. Our own additions to our bookshelves, mine and my sisters', were the books we got as gifts or the prizes we won in school. In addition to prizes for academics, participation in debates and later in quiz competitions also netted us some books as prizes in addition to trophies.

Without exception, all the prize books we received

at school were 'prescribed', in the sense that they were selected for us by teachers and they were not necessarily among our favourite reading. It was only in college in Calcutta that I realized that we could select our own prize books. St. Xavier's College (now a university) would issue us prize book coupons of a certain value redeemable at Allied Publishers on Bentinck Street, in a busy, commercial part of the city. It was a great experience to go and select books with friends (other prize-winners). The enthusiasm and pride with which we flashed our prize coupons was matched with disappointment in equal measure, when we realized that the value of the books we had selected exceeded the value of our coupons. But the books we had to have, and we managed with some extra pocket money thoughtfully provided by home, and made the proud purchase. We ensured, of course, that we had enough left over for mughlai parathas at Basant or Anandi Cabins, washed down with a cool and refreshing glass of Ralli's rose syrup.

Much later in life, and as we too downsized and got rid of our rather obsolete *Book of Knowledge* series, I was full of admiration for those 'door-to-door' book salesmen who pioneered a model that was used by the bigger book distributors successfully much later. My father had always been keen that I choose the civil services as a career path as many of my friends had done, and perhaps I was suited for it too. But I chose academics instead and my father reconciled himself by saying, 'Teaching is a noble profession.' Later, when I switched careers to join the publishing industry, he must have thought, 'Well, it has to do with books, so it can't be bad.' Or maybe he blamed those door-to-door salesmen!

My college years in Calcutta in the late 1960s were divided into two phases, one as a day scholar, commuting daily from home, and the other as a boarder in the hostel for two years. The sources of books for us now were the Park Book Bureau opposite the college for textbooks and for general reading, the Cambridge Bookshop and Oxford Books and Stationery which had a well-stocked lending library at the rear. We were on our best behaviour at the Park Book Bureau as, for one, it bordered the police station, and for another, a restrictive counter ran along the length of the very busy shop preventing you from accessing the stocks and perhaps 'purloining' them. All requirements for texts were met by the shop assistant, a 'chhotu' who knew the shelves by heart.

Which reminds me of another shop. Throughout the 1950s and 60s, statutory 'rationing' of rice, wheat, sugar and pulses prevailed and access to these commodities at government-controlled rates was through 'fair price shops' for which you needed a ration card. The card gave the names of family members and described the family as 'rice' or 'wheat' eater. As a result, you were allotted more quantities of the grain of your choice. While the quality of rice or wheat supplied was abysmal, this was the only way the urban poor could get their rations and manage to eke out an existence. A majority of middle-class families, like ours, also queued up at the ration shops because these were times of scarcity in food grains. But I soon realized that it was possible to get a slightly better quality of grain if you happened to know the shopkeeper. For a period, and in the absence of support staff, I used to collect the family rations. I was served the same fare as the others by a rather grumpy shopkeeper who had a litany of woes against the public distribution system. One day, he fell ill and the shop was managed by his son. When it came to my turn, I was intrigued to find a copy of *Mila 18* by Leon Uris beside the shopkeeper's son. We soon got into conversation on Leon Uris and the book *Exodus* and later I held forth on *Trinity*, which he had not read, and all thoughts about the rations were forgotten. When I finally remembered and expressed my concern, he served me my allotted rations from the rear of the shop, and at home that evening everyone was happy to be served a better quality of rice! My new friend informed me that sometimes the government did send a slightly superior quality of grain, but always in a limited quantity, and putting it out before the public would only invite trouble. After that, whenever I went to the shop, I was given grain from the back of the shop. Even after his father had recovered and returned to the shop, my friend continued to assist him after his classes. He was an avid reader and I rather looked forward to the ration shopping. I wouldn't have to stand in queue, and we would discuss our favourite books and authors over cups of tea. My mother used to wonder why I was such a keen 'ration-shopper' while so reluctant to accompany her on her regular shopping expeditions!

*

A glimpse at my modest library reveals more non-fiction books than fiction. Pride of place is devoted to Alberto Manguel's *A History of Reading* and *The Library at Night*. He has been a relentless crusader for books and for reading and somewhat of a mentor. I had occasion to travel to Manguel's home city, Buenos Aires, in 2010 as a UNESCO delegate to the world book capital summit meeting, to make presentations and share ideas on how we could strengthen book culture and reading, especially among children. It was thrilling to be in the city of Manguel, and that other great writer, the peerless Jorge Luis Borges. Manguel's *With Borges* describes his encounter with the iconic writer who tragically went blind in the later years of his life. Manguel first met Borges when he was sixteen and working as an assistant in the bookshop Pygmalion. Borges, almost blind already, was looking for someone to read to him as his own mother tired easily. A reluctant Manguel spent some years reading to Borges, whose passions at the time (1964) were Kipling and Robert Louis Stevenson. (Manguel himself was to later write a book on Stevenson, *Stevenson Under the Palm Trees*.)

Though in *With Borges*, Manguel recalls his years with Borges with nostalgia and warmth, in reality, he found it very difficult and laborious to read to the senior writer. For Borges had an encyclopaedic mind and constantly interrupted the reading sessions, eyes firmly shut, recalling incidents and additional information about passages just read. It was an excellent, if incidental, literary education for a precocious sixteen-year-old who hoped to be a writer, but at the time Manguel was not at all happy or grateful! His ordeal ended only when Borges engaged other readers to satisfy his growing literary appetite.

In Buenos Aires—the city with more bookshops than any other in the world—my wife and I managed to visit the National Library of Argentina. Borges had been a past director of the library and I was happy to see a special display of all his books. In a bizarre coincidence, three of the past directors of the library had gone blind (at different times). I was happy to see a bust of one of them, Jose Marmol, whose book *Amalia* I had in my collection. Today, the National Library is in safe hands. After all his traveling and wandering, Alberto Manguel has returned home to Buenos Aires and is its present director.

Two other books by Manguel adorn my shelves. One is *The City of Words* where he takes a fresh look at the rise of violent intolerance in our societies, something that seems very relevant today. Manguel says we strive to build societies that promote civic nationalism, with sets of common values that all citizens can agree upon. But something has gone terribly wrong. Manguel, with wit and erudition, asks us to look at what visionaries, poets, novelists, essayists, and filmmakers have to say about the building of our societies, and understand where and how we went wrong. The other book, *The Library at Night*, of which Yale University Press presented me a 'proof copy' at the London Book Fair many years ago, also continues to inspire me. It's a virtual tour de force on libraries through history, and the extraordinary efforts of individuals to preserve books and learning. It is Manguel's virtual tour of the history of the book. A tour extending from his childhood bookshelves to the complete libraries of the internet; from Ancient Egypt and Greece to the Arab world; from China and Rome to Google. Pondering over the personal libraries of Charles Dickens, Borges and others, he recounts stories of people who have struggled against tyranny to preserve libraries. There's an amusing story about Manguel's library at his home in Buenos Aires. His father, a diplomat, was often posted abroad. Once, ahead of his posting back to Argentina after a somewhat lengthy sojourn out of the country as ambassador, Manguel's father gave instructions to his support staff headed by an energetic housekeeper to prepare the house for the family's arrival. The heavier pieces of personal effects were sent on ahead, and these included an extensive book collection accumulated during his travels. Manguel's father instructed the staff, long distance, that the library had to be outfitted with new shelves to accommodate this treasure. The housekeeper got an army of carpenters to work on shelves and awaited the arrival of the books. When the books arrived, she found that some of them were too large for the shelves. The enterprising housekeeper, not to be deterred, got a couple of bookbinders to 'trim' the books and re-bind them. They now slipped into the shelves perfectly. Manguel writes he had a hilarious time picking up these books and trying to guess what could possibly be the last six lines now missing on every page!

No books were ever trimmed in my library. But alas, every house—indeed, the world—proves too small in the end. Henry Petroski in his history of books and their shelving, *The Book on the Bookshelf*, has said that it is but a natural law that books will in time outgrow shelves meant to house them. Perhaps, that's also why e-readers like the Kindle, the Kobo and the Sony e-reader are replacing books. But holding up a Kindle when asked to show one's library does not seem to have quite the same effect. Manguel, whose books overflowed the barn and soon began to fill up the house in the Loire in France, quotes from Julio Cortazar, another Argentinian writer. In *The House Taken Over*, Cortazar speaks of a couple who are passionate book lovers and are forced to move from room to room as each room gets filled with books. Finally, they are forced to live in the balcony as the rooms are all full.

To prevent such an eventuality, I know what the rules in our new house are. 'New books will not be taken in unless some of the old ones are given away!'

And so we lose our memories.

THE CONTINUING RELEVANCE OF AN ANCIENT APPEAL

The year 2016 marked 400 years of the passing away of the poet, playwright and actor William Shakespeare, arguably the world's greatest literary figure. The year was marked by a number of theatre performances, seminars and discussions on the dramatist. In India, Ratna Sagar Publishers decided to make Shakespeare the subject of their annual Notebook. This Notebook is a unique document. It has a topical theme every year and is distributed free-of-charge to school principals and teachers, academics, friends and well-wishers. The Notebook of 2016 was to have 16 contributions on Shakespeare, the subjects ranging from 'The World Behind the Man', 'Shakespeare and his Peers' and 'A Playwright for Every Audience', to 'Bard or Ghost', 'The Shakespearean Fool' and 'English After Shakespeare'. Each essay was to be contained within a page, with an illustration on the facing page. Invited to contribute, I resolved to steer clear of an academic topic on the Bard and instead thought I would do a piece on the story of the First Folio, the first published collection of Shakespeare's plays.

The Notebook was duly completed and distributed to

school principals and teachers to universal appreciation. Its reception indicated a continued commitment to and love for Shakespeare. But it had other consequences as well. Many of the schools indicated that Ratna Sagar surely could not stop merely with the Notebook. Could it not organize some workshops and programmes on Shakespeare that would lead to a greater appreciation and understanding of the Bard? The schools would in turn organize enactments of some iconic scenes from Shakespeare's plays. I was asked to be a part of the outreach programme and thought that I would do a presentation on the amazing story of the First Folio.

Shakespeare wrote his plays to be performed on stage and looked at them through the lens of a stage director; printing and distributing them to be read was not a priority. The first time one of his plays appeared in print was in 1594. This was his first play, *The Lamentable Tragedy of Titus Andronicus*, published in quarto format. In a quarto, each sheet was folded twice at right angles, producing four leaves of eight pages. The leaves were stitched together but the book itself was unbound. *Titus Andronicus* was printed by pirates without permission and Shakespeare's name did not appear on the title page. This was not to be the first time that Shakespeare's works had been pirated or printed anonymously, nor would it be the last.

The most famous of the unauthorized versions of Shakespeare's plays in print was the 'Pavier Quarto', printed by William Jaggard, England's leading printer at the time. It contained ten plays, including two—*Sir John*

Oldcastle and *A Yorkshire Tragedy*—which were not written by Shakespeare at all. The printed book, slightly larger than a quarto size, was sold from Thomas Pavier's bookshop. Alarmed at the interest that 'Pavier Quarto' was generating among the reading public, Shakespeare's drama company, The King's Men, which held rights to the plays, asked the Lord Chamberlain to stop its sale as their rights were being infringed upon. Their appeal was successful and led to a precedent. Hereafter, no play of Shakespeare could be printed without the permission of the shareholders of The King's Men.

On 23 April 1616, Shakespeare died at the height of his fame. He was rightly called England's greatest dramatist and had written a total of 5 long poems, 154 sonnets and 37 plays. Only half of his plays were known in a fashion, many of them pirated, corrupted and printed in a language far removed from the original. But what was even worse was that eighteen of Shakespeare's plays, including some of his greatest works, had never been published and were virtually unknown.

In his will, among other bequests, Shakespeare had left aside the sum of 26 shillings each to three of his fellow actors in The King's Men. They were Richard Burbage—the greatest actor in England at the time—John Heminges and Henry Condell. They were also fellow shareholders and actors in The King's Men. It was Shakespeare's intention that the 26 shillings be used by each of his friends to fashion gold rings so that they may remember their dear friend Will Shakespeare.

Richard Burbage died in 1620, but Heminges and

Condell conceived and thought of a more permanent way to remember their friend Will Shakespeare. Perhaps they had felt outrage at the publication of the patently false 'Pavier Quarto' in 1619 and other pirated versions. To escape scrutiny, Jaggard and Pavier had even backdated their versions. Conscious that such brazen efforts would only intensify, Heminges and Condell thought of publishing a complete record of Shakespeare's plays. This makes them two of the most unsung heroes of English literature.

It was a very laudable objective, but at that early stage, Heminges and Condell had simply no idea about the enormity of the task that lay ahead of them. They were to write later in a preface to what would become famous as the First Folio, that their objective was to compile Shakespeare's works 'without ambition of either self-profit or fame, only to keep the memory of so worthy a friend and fellow alive as was our Shakespeare'.

Heminges and Condell soon found that there was no authentic, original source for the plays. Apart from the bad, pirated versions of the earlier quartos, for eighteen of the plays no printed text, good or bad, existed at all. Shakespeare wrote out his plays as draft manuscripts. These drafts had dialogue insertions, strikeouts, emendations, substitutions and other revisions, as is usual for any written work from a first to a final draft. These drafts too, sometimes with revisions incorporated and also referred to as 'foul' copies, were then turned over to a professional scribe, Ralph Crane, who rewrote the manuscripts, thus turning 'foul' to 'fair'. But Crane performed an even more important function. He prepared manuscript 'sides' for the acting troupe. These were stand-alone fragments containing only the lines of the play to be spoken by a specific actor. There were two reasons for this. Actors were not necessarily highly educated, anything more than their own lines would have been very difficult for them to read and memorize—and even here, prompt books were developed, with prompters waiting in the wings to help out faltering actors. The second and perhaps even more important reason was that Elizabethan theatre was intensely competitive. Rival play groups pirated competitors' plays with impunity. Manuscript copies of the plays, therefore, were very few in number and kept as secret as possible.

But it was not unusual for prompt books and 'sides' with author lines to be stolen. Sometimes a popular actor would be kidnapped or spirited away by a group so as to ensure that the play would be a failure. Spies too would be sent to watch rival productions to gauge their popularity and then plots would be devised to sabotage them.

Once he had turned over the manuscripts to a scribe, Shakespeare did not retain a single original. Himself an actor, it was action on the stage that really interested him, because true success could only be gauged in the theatre. Not only would this establish his reputation as a playwright, but good gate receipts would ensure an income for him as a director in the company. So almost nothing in writing that could be verified as Shakespeare's own survived in original form. No fragment of an original manuscript—not one play, not an act, not a scene, not a single page of dialogue and not even a sentence. Even if something had somehow survived, it was certainly destroyed by the fire that devastated the Globe Theatre, the theatre built and used by The King's Men, in June 1613, three years before Shakespeare's death.

So it was a seemingly impossible task that awaited Heminges and Condell. Unfortunately, they have left no list of sources and references that they would have consulted in order to compile the First Folio. But they would have had some sources at least, or the First Folio could never have existed. Moreover, as Andrea Mays in her book *The Millionaire and the Bard* has written, 'What is lost to us today was perhaps not lost to Heminges and Condell nearly four centuries ago.' As fellow-actors in The King's Men, Heminges and Condell would have had access to more material than an ordinary researcher. Some prompt books, manuscripts sides with author lines, some stage directions etc would surely have fallen into their hands.

Moreover, eighteen (but not very authentic, and probably pirated) versions of Shakespeare's plays existed as published quartos. Heminges and Condell were able to resurrect some good quartos, like that of *Hamlet* published in 1604. Even where bad quartos existed, like the version of *Romeo and Juliet* printed in 1597, Heminges and Condell were able to use their sources to correct and produce a more authentic version. For these and other plays but more particularly for the eighteen plays that had never been published, Heminges and Condell had to rely on a unique resource—their memory. This unique resource would have helped them retain almost all they had witnessed in all of Shakespeare's plays enacted on the stage. As actors, they would have rehearsed their lines, seen their fellow-actors recite their lines and above all, seen Shakespeare himself act and even direct. Human memory though ephemeral and somewhat unreliable, is still the richest and most valuable record of history, and Heminges's and Condell's would have served them well, especially as it would have still been fresh when they set about compiling the First Folio.

Even so, the front page of the First Folio which stated 'Mr William Shakespeares Comedies, Histories & Tragedies, Publithed according to the True Originall Copies' was stretching things a little! It took years of dedicated and hard labour for Heminges and Condell to compile thirty-six of Shakespeare's plays. They cleared publishing rights from both the Stationer's Company and The King's Men. They were unable to clear rights for *Troilus and Cressida* and *Pericles* and these were not in the original collection. However, before printing, *Troilus and Cressida* was granted a reprieve and thus *Pericles* remains the sole play not included in the First Folio.

The plays were not the only material that Heminges and Condell included in the First Folio. They solicited authors, from minor poets to big names like Shakespeare's illustrious friend, author and playwright Ben Jonson, to write memorial poems. Jonson's composition was a remarkable eulogy, and he prefaced this with a most memorable dedication to his dear friend William

Shakespeare: 'He was not of an Age but for All Time.' Heminges and Condell themselves made four contributions to the preliminary pages. A catalogue of all the plays included a roster of the principal actors who performed in them, a dedication and a memorial essay, a personal tribute to their friend. The dedication was 'To the Most Noble & Incomparable Paire of Brethren, William, Earl of Pembroke, Lord Chamberlaine to the King's Most Excellent Majesty and Philip, Earl of Pembroke and Montgomery'. They were two nobles from whom Heminges and Condell hoped to receive patronage to defray the huge printing costs.

As the text was being finalized, Heminges and Condell thought up another, entirely novel feature. This was the inclusion of the author's image in the First Folio. For the first time in the history of English literature, an author's portrait would be carried prominently on the title page. It was almost as if Heminges and Condell were saying, 'You cannot just have the words; you must behold the man.' Thus we have the only authentic—or near authentic—portrait of Shakespeare. For this, Heminges and Condell did not commission a cheap, crude woodcut. They wanted to have their friend's portrait engraved on a copper plate to achieve a more accurate and direct likeness.

This illustration, the only one in the book, was executed by the twenty-two-year-old Flemish engraver Martin Droeshout. Droeshout must have been too young to have seen Shakespeare in the flesh. In part, he must have based his portrait on some pre-existing source, a sketch or a painting long lost, and in part it must have also been based on an accurate, realistic and vivid description of Shakespeare by Heminges and Condell. A further testimony to their extraordinary memory, descriptive skills and professional and personal integrity in their project. Engravers were copyists, after all.

When at last the text was ready, Heminges and Condell had ironically to approach William Jaggard to print copies. It was the same Jaggard who had printed the pirated 'Pavier Quarto'. But he was the best equipped printer in London at the time. At any rate, he was an old man and in the two years that it took to print the copies, Jaggard became blind and his son Isaac took over the printing. The book was to be sold by Edward Blount at his shop, The Sign of the Black Bear, in St. Paul's Churchyard. Isaac Jaggard and Edward Blount appeared as the printer and bookseller in the First Folio, and they in fact now owned it and controlled all rights.

It took two years for Jaggard to print 750 copies, the number 750 having been arrived at as the most viable for the bookseller to make a profit. The printing was finally completed in 1623, seven years after Shakespeare had passed away. The book was printed in unbound sheets and patrons could buy the sheets and have them bound in parchment, goatskin or calfskin. Heminges and Condell had also included in the preliminary pages an appeal to 'the great Variety of Readers, to read and censure but buy it first'. They also wanted the public to gaze at the portrait of their dear friend William Shakespeare, 'whose mind and hand went together. And what he thought, he uttered with that easinesse, that we have scarse received from him a blot in his papers'. That Shakespeare could move his hand so quickly across the page that his quill did not leave a blot was, too, an exaggeration, but it could be excused on the ground that Heminges and Condell wanted to prove that Shakespeare was indeed the author of the plays. And they urged the reader, again, to find in the text 'enough, both to draw and hold you for his wit can no more lie hid, than it could be lost. Reade him therefore, and againe and againe but whatever you do, Buy'.

This appeal by the two finds echoes to the present day, where poor publishers silently—or not so silently, at their book launches—and hopefully beseech the public 'to buy'. It was not a very hopeful task back in 1623 (as, indeed, it isn't even today). By no means was the First Folio a bestseller. Not all the printed sheets were purchased to be bound into books. Today, 235 copies of the First Folio survive, 80 of which are in the Folger Shakespeare Library in Washington.

I recounted the story of the First Folio to a group of senior principals from the leading schools of Hyderabad at the Microsoft office facility a few years ago. After the talk, the principals enacted the courtroom scene from *The Merchant of Venice*. Concluding the session, I took my cue from the principals' performance and marvelled at Shakespeare's accurate portrayal of anti-Semitism in *The Merchant of Venice*. When Shylock says 'suffering is the badge of our tribe' in 1590, Shakespeare with miraculous prescience is anticipating that the Star of David would become the visible badge of suffering for a beleaguered community so many years later. More recently, their lordships Madan Lokur and Deepak Gupta of the Indian Supreme Court had lamented in a judgement that the life of the migrant workers in the construction industry was like 'a Shakespeare tragedy'. Their lordships were referring to the fact that funds meant for the welfare of the workers were largely lying unused. That term, 'Shakespeare tragedy', would have remained unknown in our history but for the labours of the unsung heroes of English literature, John Heminges and Henry Condell, Without their efforts, Shakespeare's tragedies, as indeed his comedies, would have disappeared into oblivion with his death.

AN INDIAN AUTHOR AND ENTREPRENEUR IN ENGLAND

DEAN MAHOMED (1759-1851)

When, in early 2019, Google carried a doodle celebrating a somewhat unusual Indian-British man called Dean Mahomed, I was pleasantly surprised. Few people outside India's literary and quizzing circles would have heard of Dean Mahomed. And his achievements, too, were not of the kind that are normally considered worthy of celebration—he did not invent a world-changing gadget, or score 100 test centuries, or set up a global business empire. But he did, in his small and surprising way, expand the definition of enterprise, migration, entrepreneurship and autobiographical writing.

My mind went back to the London Book Fair of 2010. Travelling around the city after I had finished my appointments, I came across a blue plaque that said 'Hindostanee Coffee House'. It marked a site at the corner of George and Charles Streets where the coffee house once stood. It was a quiet little memorial to an intrepid Indian entrepreneur who had not only established the coffee house, thus being a forerunner of Indian cuisine in

England, but was also—and more famously—responsible for pioneering 'Indian therapy' in England. He was also able to show scientifically the beneficial results of his therapy at a time when evidence-based research was in its infancy. Dean Mahomed pioneered the art of shampooing and massaging in England by setting up the first shampooing parlour there. The beneficial effects of this therapy—a clever re-imagining of tel-maalish and champi—became so popular that Mahomed came to be known as a 'shampooing surgeon', though he had no formal degree in medicine. He also kept a diary, a record of his travels and adventures in India, Ireland and England and later published them in two volumes, thus becoming the first Indian author in English.

Dean Mahomed's life is a wonderful story of determination and adventure—and rare business acumen. Dean ('Deen', before the Anglicization), was born in Patna, the son of a barber (therefore the prowess in maalish and champi). This was the period of the slow dissolution of the once mighty Mughal empire, and the East India Company was making inroads into previous Mughal strongholds. By the middle of the eighteenth century, the Company had made a decisive change both in its incorporation and in its character. It was now no longer a mere trading company; it had begun to assume a very significant administrative presence with a strong military character. The Company needed native volunteers as sepoys and those recruited into service began to be known as 'Company bahadurs'. Dean Mahomed's family decided that the family's future and loyalties lay with the Company. Accordingly, both Mahomed's father and elder brother joined the Company's Bengal Army. As for Mahomed himself, he was apprenticed at the age of eleven to an Anglo-Irish patron, Ensign Godfrey Evan Baker, who took a shine to the ambitious young boy. During the next eleven years, Mahomed saw service in the military campaigns of the Bengal Army along with Baker, and as Baker rose to become captain with his own independent command, Mahomed too was promoted regularly, becoming a master and then a subaltern officer. He travelled extensively in the service of the Bengal Army, and apart from Bihar, Oudh and Benares, visited Calcutta, Delhi and Madras.

Finally, in 1784, Mahomed gave up his Company job and set sail for England along with his benefactor Baker and landed in Cork via Dartmouth. He was to spend almost the next twenty-five years of his life in Cork, gaining a measure of respectability among the Anglo-Irish society and learning and perfecting English. As his English improved, Mahomed began to write poetry too as this was an accepted part of the cultured life of the Irish elite. In 1786, he married an Irish girl, Jane Daly, somewhat in haste and in secret. He had converted to Protestantism and Jane was a Catholic and marriage between the faiths was forbidden at the time. Dean Mahomed was a trusted friend of the entire Baker household and at that time was engaged in commercial activity, initially trading in the large number of goods that Baker and he had brought out from India by ship.

How do we know so much about Mahomed's early

life? He kept a diary of his travels and adventures in India and the voyage to England and his early days there. In March 1793 he resolved to publish it as a book in two volumes. The economics of publishing at that time was that no printer would undertake a book's printing even with advance payment unless it was subscribed for. No printer wanted to stock any books, either bound copies or loose sheets. Subscription ensured that copies would move out to the subscribers immediately upon printing. In this, Mahomed was greatly helped by Baker's extended family, who subscribed for a total of 112 copies. Thus, in 1794, Mahomed's *Travels* was published, making him the first Indian author in English. In India, we are indebted to the historian Michael Fisher, then of Oberlin College, who discovered Mahomed's *Travels* and presented it with an extensive analysis and commentary as *Dean Mahomed (1759-1851) in India, Ireland and England.*

In 1807, Mahomed and Jane along with their children migrated to London. He found service with a controversial nobleman, Basil Cochrane, in Portman Square. Cochrane had learned the therapeutic effects of vapour cure while in service in India and had now thought of setting up a vapour bath in his house. He invited Dean Mohamed to help him set up the bath. While Turkish baths or hamams had been introduced in London as far back as 1631, the therapeutic effects of vapour had mainly been confined to discussions in medical circles. It had not yet been commercially exploited. So Basil Cochrane's idea was an entirely novel one.

While the original idea came from Cochrane, it was

Dean Mahomed who set up the first vapour bath. He also perfected the idea of applying medicated steam to various parts of the body. By the end of 1809, Mahomed felt confident of launching his own business, using his Indian identity as his calling card. He established the Hindostanee Coffee House at the corner of George and Charles Streets and offered to his patrons a unique Indian experience. The house served a range of meat and vegetable dishes cooked with Indian spices, served with seasoned rice. Seating was on bamboo cane sofas and chairs, on the walls were paintings of Indian landscapes, and for discerning patrons there was a smoking room with 'hookahs with scented tobacco and Indian herbs'. And of course, Mahomed did not serve coffee but only wines and other spirits! The Hindostanee Coffee House ran from 1810 to 1812, the ancestor of all the many Indian eating establishments that flourish in London today.

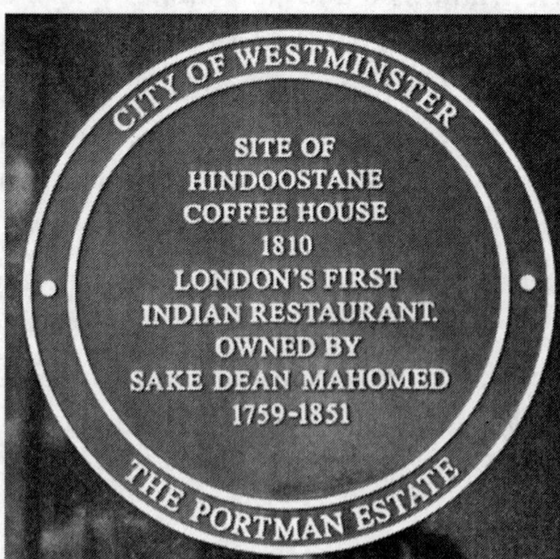

It was Dean Mahomed's move to Brighton in 1813 to set up the Mahomed Baths that finally established his reputation—primarily as a 'therapist'. Besides vapour baths, Mahomed also added shampooing to his repertoire, and shampooing here meant the expert art of oil massage, or maalish. The baths were a runaway success, and Mahomed became quite famous as a shampooing surgeon. Advertisements for the Indian medicated vapour and shampooing baths proclaimed their curative powers in rheumatism, paralysis, asthma, gout, stiff joints and sprain. In 1820, Mahomed's reputation was further strengthened by his book *Shampooing; or Benefits resulting from the use of the Indian medicated vapour bath*, which explained his famed methods. A second edition of the book was published in 1826.

Mahomed dedicated the book to King George, who along with William IV patronized Mahomed's baths. The Duke of Wellington was also a patron, along with other members of the royal household. However, Queen Victoria declined her patronage, which perhaps led to a dip in the reputation of the Mahomed Baths.

Unfortunately, Mahomed's sons failed to run the baths properly amid growing competition. Mahomed eventually lost control of the baths in his lifetime. He died in his eighties and was buried in Brighton in 1851.

'IS SHANGHAI ON THE WAY TO BOMBAY?'

Three leading English publishing firms set up offices in India at the end of the nineteenth and beginning of the twentieth centuries. These were Longman Green, which established a sales depot in 1895, followed by Macmillan, and finally by Oxford University Press, which opened an office in Bombay in 1912. This was to consolidate and nurture a growing market for English books in India developed by travelling salesmen of English firms. The reading public was, of course, both the official English as well as the non-official English who were starved of adequate reading material in India. But what gave publishers greater hope and encouragement was the growing class of Indian readers eager to take advantage of English as a medium of instruction following Macaulay's famous Minute on Education in 1835.

By all means, Emile Victor Rieu (1887-1972) was a curious choice to head the Indian operations of OUP. He was a scholar and academic trained in the classics, and not, at least visibly, a business or management mind. But he was a product of Baliol, an 'Oxford man', and that was all that mattered to Humphrey Milford, the Oxford

Publisher, who took almost three years to find the ideal candidate in Rieu. And when he did, he asked Rieu, 'Is Shanghai on the way to Bombay?' 'Yes, if one goes by the Trans-Siberian Railway,' replied Rieu.

In case one thinks a lesson in geography might have been in order, let me explain that Milford had wanted Rieu to go out to Bombay via Shanghai for a purpose. He was dissatisfied with OUP's agent in Shanghai and wanted Rieu to check and, if necessary, sack him. Which Rieu dutifully did. Rieu then reached Bombay in September 1912 and set up the OUP office on Hornby Road. For the record, Rieu had travelled to India the previous year on a reconnaissance and market survey for OUP and based on meetings with other representatives of publishers, including Edmund Marsden, the manager of Macmillan in India, concluded that there was indeed a market for books in the subcontinent. He also determined that Bombay would be the choice for OUP's office in India.

Milford gave the OUP managers quite a bit of autonomy and freedom to operate and Rieu vindicated his trust. He gradually grew OUP's business, initially in the area of school textbooks. Among the first academic books that were published was *Essentials of Psychology* by a then young and comparatively unknown lecturer in philosophy, Sarvepalli Radhakrishnan. Radhakrishnan was, of course, to achieve fame later, first as the Spalding Professor of Eastern Religions and Ethics at Oxford and later as Vice President and President of India.

Rieu made a trip back to England in 1914 to get married. The newlyweds had to cut short their honeymoon and return to India as war had already broken out. Moreover, Hugh Cass, Rieu's assistant, had resigned to join military service. Shortly after returning to Bombay, learning that his three brothers had been killed in action in France, Rieu asked for and was given permission to sign up for service and received a commission to join the 105th Maratha Light Infantry. In answer to Milford's query as to who would run the branch in his absence, Rieu said, 'My wife!' And so it was that Nellie Rieu ran OUP India for two years, her earlier stint at Edwin Arnold in London standing her well, until Rieu returned to office in 1918 almost at the end of the war.

A week before Armistice Day, Rieu had to solve the urgent problem of shifting the Bombay office. The landlord had given notice that they had outgrown the space on the first floor and moreover, he feared the weight of the stock of books would put too heavy a load on the floor. Rieu, realizing that the growing weight of books would indeed pose a problem, found suitable premises on the ground floor at Elphinstone Circle. The premises came along with a basement which was ideal for warehousing stock. What the new landlord failed to mention was that the premises came along with an indolent cow which took up a leisurely position at the entrance on most afternoons. Nothing would make the cow move from its habitat, nor did the office goers try very hard to move the gentle animal. The more nimble footed did a hop, skip and jump over the animal to reach the stairs. Sales staff who found this exercise arduous spent the whole day on field visits. There is no record of the savings to OUP on a security guard on account of the diligence of the vigilant cow!

Reasons of health forced Rieu to return to England in 1919. He was succeeded as manager by Geoffrey Cumberlege who would soon rise to become the Publisher at Oxford. Indeed, a stint in India was considered very good training for the OUP managers, and one of them, A.L.P. Norrington, subsequently became Vice Chancellor of the University of Oxford.

Rieu himself was to achieve fame as a translator of the classics. He translated Homer's *Iliad* and *Odyssey* from Greek. His knowledge of both Latin and Greek was to prove very useful and he soon became the general editor of the Penguin Classics in 1944, and remained in the position for twenty years. He was so absorbed in his work that it is rumoured he even ignored calls to take refuge in the underground shelter during the London bombings of World War II.

What is perhaps not so widely known is that Rieu was also a remarkable writer of verse for children. In his poetry, his humour and sympathy for children is evident. 'Hall and Knight' was a poem that Rieu wrote to record his sympathy for the generations of schoolchildren who had to endure Hall and Knight's 'Algebra', which was the standard textbook in mathematics.

Hall and Knight or 'z+b+x = y+b+z

When he was young his cousins used to say of Mr Knight
'This boy will write an algebra—or looks as if he might.'
And sure enough, when Mr Knight had grown to be a man,
He purchased pen and paper and an inkpot, and began.

But he very soon discovered that he couldn't write at all,
And his heart was filled with yearnings for a certain Mr Hall;
Till, after many years of doubt, he sent his friend a card
'Have tried to write an Algebra, but find it very hard.'

Now Mr Hall himself had tried to write a book for schools,
But suffered from a handicap, he didn't know the rules.
So when he heard from Mr Knight and understood his gist,
He answered him by telegram 'Delighted to assist.'

So Mr Hall and Mr Knight they took a house together,
And they worked away at algebra in any kind of weather,
Determined not to give up until they had evolved
A problem so constructed that it never could be solved.

'How hard it is,' said Mr Knight, 'to hide the fact from youth
that x and y are equal; it is such an obvious truth!'
'It is,' said Mr Hall, 'but if we gave a b to each,
We'd put the problem well beyond our little victims' reach.

'Or are you anxious, Mr Knight, lest any boy should see
The utter superfluity of this repeated b.'
'I scarcely fear it,' he replied, and scratched his grizzled head,
'But perhaps it would be safer if to b we added z.'

'A brilliant stroke,' said Hall, and added z to either side;
Then looked at his accomplice with a flush of happy pride.
And Knight, he winked at Hall (a very pardonable lapse).
And they printed off the Algebra and sold it to the chaps.

Thus, Rieu as a scholar of the classics showed his disdain for mathematics and his sympathy for a multitude of schoolchildren who had to grapple with the intricacies of Hall and Knight's 'Algebra'.

But Hall and Knight live on. Their books continue to sell and their Higher Algebra is still used as a text for the joint entrance examination in engineering studies in India!

Rieu wrote many other memorable poems for young readers. Like 'Sir Smasham Uppe', which depicts the eccentricities and clumsiness of an absentminded noble, thus revealing Rieu's sneaking sympathy for children who are all thumbs and butter fingers and a bundle of nerves.

Sir Smasham Uppe

Good afternoon, Sir Smasham Uppe,
We're having tea; do take a cup.
Sugar and milk? Now let me see
Two lumps I think?...Good gracious me!
The silly thing slipped off your knee?
Pray don't apologize, old chap

A very trivial mishap.
So clumsy of you? How absurd!
My dear Sir Smasham, not a word.

Now do sit down and have another,
And tell us all about your brother—
You know, the one who broke his head.
Is the poor fellow still in bed?

A chair? Allow me sir,...Great Scott!
That was a nasty smash! Eh, what?
Oh, not at all; the chair was old—
Queen Anne, or so we have been told.
We've got at least a dozen more.
Just leave the pieces on the floor.

I want you to admire our view.
Come nearer to the window, do.
And look how beautiful...Tut, tut!
You didn't see that it was shut?
I hope you are not badly cut?
Not hurt? A fortunate escape!
Amazing! Not a single scrape!

And now, if you have finished tea,
I fancy you might like to see
A little thing or two I've got.
That china plate? Yes, worth a lot.
A beauty too...Ah there it goes!
I trust it didn't hurt your toes?

Your elbow brushed it off the shelf?
Of course, I've done the same myself.
And now, my dear Sir Smasham—Oh!

You surely don't intend to go?
You must be off? Well, come again
So glad you're fond of porcelain!

In the end, it will be Rieu's achievements as a translator of classics and, perhaps even more, his poetry that he will be remembered for best even a hundred years from now. His most enduring poem may well be 'The Unicorn', which evokes brilliantly the imaginative spirit of children and their yearning for the magical and the mystical. Today, 'The Unicorn' has become a school song in the UK and is also a term for start-ups (as OUP India was more than a century ago), symbolizing the hopes and dreams of their founders.

The Unicorn

The Unicorn stood, like a king in a dream,
On the bank of a dark Senegambian stream;
And flaming flamingoes flew over his head,
As the African sun rose in purple and red.

Who knows what the thoughts of a unicorn are
When he shines on the world like a rising star;
When he comes from the magical pages of a story
In the pride of his horn and a halo of glory?

He followed the paths where the jungle beasts go,
And he walked with a step that was stately and slow;
But he threw not a shadow and made not a sound,
And his foot was as light as the wind on the ground.

The lion looked up with his terrible eyes,
And growled like the thunder to hide his surprise.

He thought for a while, with a paw in the air;
Then tucked up his tail and turned into his lair.

The gentle giraffe ran away to relate
The news to his tawny and elegant mate,
While the snake slid aside with a venomous hiss,
And the little birds piped: 'There is something amiss!'

And the Unicorn strode with his head in a cloud
And uttered his innocent fancies aloud.
'What a wonderful world!' he was heard to exclaim;
'It is better than books: it is sweeter than fame!'

And he gazed at himself, with a thrill and a quiver,
Reflected in white by the slow-flowing river.
'O speak to me, dark Senegambian stream,
And prove that my beauty is more than a dream!'

He had paused for a word in the midst of his pride,
When a whisper came down through the leaves at his side
From a spying, malevolent imp of an ape
With a twist in his tail and a villainous shape.

'He was made by the stroke of a fanciful pen;
He was wholly invented by ignorant men.
One word in his ear, and one puff of the truth—
And a unicorn fades in the flower of his youth.'

The Unicorn heard and the demon of doubt
Crept into his heart, and the sun was put out.
He looked in the water, but saw not a gleam
In the slow-flowing deep Senegambian stream.

He turned to the woods, and his shadowy form
Was seen through the trees like the moon in a storm.

And the darkness fell down on the Gambian plain;
And the stars of the Senegal sought him in vain.

He had come like a beautiful melody heard
When the strings of the fiddle are tunefully stirred;
And he passed where the splendours of melody go
When the hand of the fiddler surrenders the bow.

A LEGEND CALLED HAWK

ROY HAWKINS (1907-1990)

India, as we have noted before, was a very good training ground for most of the expatriate managers sent out to oversee the Oxford University Press operations in India. Most of them went back to higher positions in the Press in Oxford, like Geoffrey Cumberlege, who became the Secretary to the Delegates, or A.L.P. Norrington, who later became the Vice Chancellor of the University of Oxford. Rieu, of course, was picked up by Allen Lane to become chief editor of the Penguin Classics series. But there was one outstanding manager of the Press in India who did not quite go back except for a few occasional trips. This was Roy Hawkins, who joined OUP in India under some very curious circumstances.

The historian and biographer Ram Guha, at the release of his wonderful biography of the British anthropologist Verrier Elwin, *Savaging the Civilized*, said that for dedicated people like Verrier Elwin, Salim Ali and Jim Corbett, there was simply no return ticket from the forest. To this list, in the context of publishing, we can add the name of Roy Hawkins who came out to India from England in 1930 and never really went back.

In 1930, India was not quite a forest, though it was seething with nationalist sentiment, as Gandhi had just launched the non-cooperation movement. Gandhi and India's national movement were to become instrumental, almost by accident, in Hawkins's eventual career choice.

Born to nonconformist parents in 1907, Hawkins passed out of Oxford, majoring in French, in 1928. He was intrigued by Gandhi while reading Fulop Miller's *Lenin and Gandhi* at university. He was to say later that the image of the Dandi March—of Gandhi accompanied by thousands of his followers clad in white—had completely captured his imagination. Hawkins had come to India in the year of the Dandi March, having managed to secure with the help of the eminent educationist, reformer and friend of Gandhi, C.F. Andrews, an appointment to join the staff of a school to be opened in Delhi. But he soon learned that the school could not be opened as the nationalist movement was in full swing and Delhi was a hotbed of political activity. A disappointed Hawkins later wrote to Madeleine Slade (Mira Behn) for permission to join Gandhi at Sabarmati Ashram. Mira Behn wrote back to say that this was not a good time, for everyone was caught up in the excitement of the nationalist struggle and the Ashram itself might soon be empty. Moreover, Gandhi himself was away from Sabarmati, leading the struggle, and Hawkins as a first-time Englishman in India would require training and guidance. She asked Hawkins to bide his time and wait for the present crisis to be over.

However, an impatient Hawkins was not one to wait. He travelled to Bombay and joined the OUP office as an assistant to Raymond Goffin, who had succeeded Cumberlege as manager. Goffin had been teaching at Cotton College in Gauhati before joining the Press; it was quite a change and he needed the help. Rimi Chatterjee in her well-researched account of the early history of OUP in India, *Empires of the Mind: A History of the Oxford University Press in India Under the Raj*, has a curious theory. She feels Hawkins was a bit like 'the spy who came in from the cold'. While researching the archives in England in the course of writing the book, Chatterjee had come across a packet of papers that once belonged to Hawkins. In it were twenty-four reports or bulletins prepared between 1930-31, containing detailed and meticulous accounts of Congress meetings, agitations, strikes, riots, rumours and propaganda in Bombay. Chatterjee speculates that the reports were part of the updates detailing the circumstances under which OUP operated in India that Hawkins sent to Humphrey Milford, who was still the Secretary in Oxford. But speculating further, Chatterjee also says that the reports were so detailed and extensive, that they went far beyond the proper requirements of what was needed by OUP, Oxford, for its publishing operations in India. She then intriguingly asks the question, 'Who were these reports for and what was their purpose?' But then she back-pedals a bit and remarks that nothing overmuch need be made of this, for the British used a whole lot of sources to gather intelligence in India and Hawkins was just one minor source.

Be that as it may, people who worked with Hawkins

in OUP noticed that he seemed to hold two seemingly paradoxical positions. On the one hand, a close identification with the nationalist sentiments prevalent in India, and on the other, a belief that the English had an overall civilizing influence in India and that not everything the Congress did was right. At the same time, Hawkins certainly did not identify himself with the hard-core imperialists back home, the 'Churchillians'. During his long stint with OUP in India, we can safely assume that the 'nationalist' sentiment in Hawkins won over the 'imperialist'.

Years later, I was to ask two senior colleagues in OUP who had worked closely with Hawkins, or 'Hawk' as he came to be known in the Press, for their views on the matter. Ravi Dayal, who was with OUP for twenty-six years, retiring as the head in 1987, firmly believed that Hawk had identified himself with India closely. In spite of his own personal difficulties in working with a man as fastidious and exacting as Hawk, Ravi felt he had become 'Indian' in spirit. However, Neil O'Brien, recruited by Hawk in 1964, and who also rose to head OUP, believed that there was indeed a bit of the imperialist in Hawk.

Neil did not give concrete reasons for his assessment of Hawk. But as I write this, I am reminded of a meeting of the OUP in Bombay in 1989. After the meeting that day, a sightseeing trip had been arranged to the Borivili National Park and the Aarey Milk Colony with dinner at the Sea Princess Hotel in Juhu. Neil asked me if I intended going on the trip. Sensing an intent behind the question, I answered no and explained that I was going to take a nap before joining everyone for dinner. Neil asked me if I knew the way to get to Juhu. Intrigued, I said yes. Neil then had a proposition. Would it be possible for me to show him the flat that Hawk had occupied and the road on which he had stayed? I said I would, for Hawk had stayed at Valentina on Gamadia Road and it was on our way via Pedder Road. Neil wanted to have a Chinese lunch and we went to Nanking opposite the Gateway. It was a sumptuous lunch and Neil's treat. On the way to Juhu, I asked the cab to go via Gamadia Road and pointed out Hawk's flat in Valentina. Neil looked up and asked, 'But wasn't there a house here before?' I said yes, there had been a bungalow earlier where Hawk had lived, but it was later pulled down to make apartments and Hawk had been given one. Only then did it dawn on me that in the six years that Neil worked with Hawk, albeit in Calcutta, never once had Hawk invited him to the house. Surely, there would have been more than at least one meeting in Bombay in those six years? It wasn't as if Hawk did not entertain at home, he often did. And this when Neil was deputy manager, and a man who gave so generously of his own hospitality at his home both in Calcutta and later in Delhi.

Coming back to Hawk's career with OUP, he succeeded Raymond Goffin as manager in 1937 and the post was upgraded to that of general manager in 1940. During his long years at the Press, Hawk led OUP to achieve pre-eminent status in both academic and educational publishing. Along the way, he forged exemplary relationships both on the personal and professional front with a group of truly great writers. Among them were Verrier Elwin, Jim Corbett, Salim Ali, K.P.S. Menon and Minoo Masani. Some of the books Hawk commissioned stood the test of time and have become standard reference material over the years. Many of them continue to be in print even today. Salim Ali's *Handbook of the Birds of India and Pakistan* grew into ten volumes, the tenth volume being released after Hawk's retirement. Jim Corbett's *Man-Eaters of the Kumaon*, an unsolicited manuscript first published in 1944, is in print even today along with all of Corbett's other books. OUP published the 25th impression of *The Man-Eaters of Kumaon* in 2003 and the then publishing history of the book on the title-verso said it all: 'First published in 1944, second edition in 1945, published in the Champak Library edition in 1947, an educational edition also in 1947, reprinted in 1949, 1952, 1955, 1959, 1963, 1969, first Indian paperback edition in 1979, published in Oxford India Paperbacks in 1988 and so on to 2003.' In addition, the book has been translated into a number of Indian and foreign languages (14 European and 11 Indian) and published both in the US and in the UK. It has also been made into a Hollywood film by Universal Pictures starring Monty Shaff and Sabu.

Corbett's original manuscript, titled *Jungle Stories*, had been read and re-read by Hawk several times. He felt it showed promise but just to be sure, got it read by a friend who also liked it. As Corbett had more stories from the jungle, it was Hawk who made the final selection for the book. He also got Corbett to revise and tighten up some of the stories. In a letter to Corbett dated 15 October 1943, Hawk had stated, 'The public is hard to please and—like other game—seldom gives a second chance.' Corbett himself was to quote this line back to Hawk when the latter complained that Corbett's pictures of tigers were all dead tigers. Corbett had replied that if any of the pictures had been of a 'live' tiger, he himself would have been dead, for a tiger seldom gave a second chance!

It was Hawk's promotion of *The Man-Eaters of Kumaon* in the US that led to it being chosen as a 'Book of the Month' by the Book Club Association, and a glitzy launch in New York. The book would go on to sell 489,000 copies in the US. And Hawk would go on to edit *Jim Corbett's India* for the Press.

OUP witnessed steady growth in India during the 'Hawk years', as the chapter on India in volume 111 (1896-1970) of *A History of Oxford University Press* (general editor Simon Elliott) has shown. Hawk also—without meaning to, I'd imagine—helped other presses grow. As Ravi Dayal had stated in an obituary article on Hawk ('A Publisher's Guru', published in *India Week* in 1990), 'Hawkins trained a whole crop of young publishers who worked with him [and] trained others who frequently carried the skills and methods learned from Hawk to other firms and regions.'

Hawk was poorly sighted and almost blind in one eye. But this did not come in the way of his editing manuscripts and making notes in detail. Nor in his other pursuits. He had a great love for the outdoors and used to spend days hiking in the Western Ghats. He was an early member of the Bombay History Natural Society (BNHS) and edited the *Encyclopaedia of Indian Natural History*, a joint imprint of the BNHS and OUP. He also contributed to the *Himalayan Journal* and helped set up hiking and mountaineering clubs. Hawk's manner could at times intimidate people and his quest for perfection could border on idiosyncrasy. He would clamber up stepladders to check stock during stocktaking. Once, on checking copies on display, he found a particular book missing. He told all the staff about the missing book and gave a chance for the miscreant to own up. No one came forward. Later, Hawk found that the book had come back to the shelf. Hawk said nothing in public, but later that day a young colleague was called in to his office and severely reprimanded. The man was bewildered as to how he had been found out. Apparently, Hawk had examined the returned book and found the stub of a bus ticket in its pages. He knew the routes the staff used to take to reach home. He thus narrowed down his list of culprits, and then a few strong words established the truth!

On that ride from Gamadia Road to Juhu to see Hawk's flat in 1989, Neil O'Brien told me the story of his recruitment to the Calcutta office of OUP. Satisfying himself on other parameters, Hawk finally wanted to test Neil's knowledge of Bengali. There was only one dilemma. Hawk did not know the language beyond a few basics. So he called in the office head clerk, the 'burra babu', and without telling him anything of the context, instructed him to pose a few questions in Bengali to Neil.

The babu did so dutifully and Neil replied fluently. Hawk was satisfied and Neil got the job. But the poor babu was left quite mystified. After Neil had joined OUP, the babu confided that he had thought Neil was an inspector from the sales tax department who did not know English!

*

Hawk, during his long tenure of thirty years as general manager of OUP in India, oversaw all operations of the Press—academic and school publishing, the small vernacular publishing programme, operations in the head office in Bombay and the branch offices in Chennai and Calcutta, and trade with the Oxford and New York offices. To perhaps relieve Hawk from some of his duties, especially in the later years, Charles Lewis was sent out from Oxford to become the Bombay manager. But Hawk remained as 'hands on' as before. Not only did he nurture authors who became longstanding writers for the Press, he also recruited staff who would serve OUP in India for many years to come. Prominent among them was Neil O'Brien, recruited in 1964, who was to succeed the long-serving R.L. Sen as manager in Calcutta and go on to eventually become the managing director of OUP India. Hawk finally retired in 1970, after having the satisfaction of seeing the Press achieve pre-eminent status in India.

Some days after Hawk passed away, I sent a copy of Ravi's obituary piece, 'A Publisher's Guru', to Sharad Patel, who had been Hawk's companion and friend in his later years. Hawk had never remarried after an unhappy marriage which ended after his wife left him to return to

England. Sharad sent me a reply in her own hand from her Pedder Road apartment. She was quite distraught at Hawk's demise, for her association with Hawk had been long. She thanked me for sending Ravi's article and asked me to thank him for his nice sentiments on Hawk. She said it had been quite a wrench going through Hawk's things and death was 'so, so, final'. Nothing really prepared anyone for the death of a loved one.

I showed Ravi Sharad's letter. He shared an anecdote about Hawk's flat in Bombay, which Sharad frequented. 'You know, Hawk's flat was a literary and artists' salon in the early days,' he told me. Apparently, Souza, Ara, Gaitonde, Hussain and other artists and some theatre activists from the Indian People's Theatre Organization (IPTA) would meet regularly at Hawk's flat. Debates on India's future would rage furiously while the artists sketched, discarded what they had sketched and sketched again, with Hawk all the while playing host, sometimes helped by Sharad. I was intrigued, for it added another dimension to Hawk. Some years later, I met the veteran artist Krishan Khanna on the sidelines of the launch of Yashodara Dalmia's *The Oxford History of Progressive Indian Art* at the British Council in Delhi. I asked Krishan about the Progressive Artists meeting in Hawk's flat. Krishan was incredulous. 'How do you know this?' he asked. I mentioned Ravi and he nodded. 'You know, I too used to be there sometimes. But I was a subaltern working with the Grindlays Bank in Bombay. As such, I would be confined to the balcony.' Krishan confirmed that sketches would be made and discarded as waste. 'If only some of that "waste" had been preserved!'

Rimi Chatterjee in her history of OUP India has written that beneath his rough exterior, Hawk was known to be quite amiable and possessed a sense of humour. Nowhere was this more evident than at the launch of the tenth volume of *The Handbook of Indian Birds* at the residence of the then Prime Minister Indira Gandhi in New Delhi. Hawk had come down from Bombay for the occasion. He regaled Mrs Gandhi with a poem:

William Shakespeare's a master of words,
And a tusker a leader of herds.
But wherever you fare,
Over, land, sea or air,
Salim Ali's the raja of birds!

The photograph taken on the occasion shows a beaming Mrs Gandhi with Hawk along with Salim Ali and Ravi Dayal. Possibly the only occasion when both Salim and Ravi sported a jacket and a tie!

TIGERS CAN ACT

There was a young lady of Riga,
Who smiled as she rode on a tiger;
They returned from the ride
With the lady inside,
And the smile on the face of the tiger!

Can a tiger smile? The noted writer and bestselling author Ruskin Bond posed this question some years ago in his column 'Musings from the Mountains'. At best, Ruskin felt, a tiger could give a satisfied snarl. While making this observation, Ruskin also digressed to the subject of man-eating tigers, and to the legendary hunter and wildlife expert Jim Corbett. Ruskin wrote that Corbett was at heart a conservationist and lover of wildlife and wanted to protect the animals and their habitat. He only killed a tiger when it had become a man-eater. It is circumstances that compel a tiger to become a man-eater when it cannot find natural prey or becomes too old to hunt. But once it has tasted human flesh, there is no turning back. 'It was possible for a human non-vegetarian to turn vegetarian but not the tiger,' noted Ruskin. Humans were easy prey and the craving for their flesh was so overpowering that the tiger would attack repeatedly. Thus Corbett was called upon both by the state and local villagers to hunt down man-eaters who had spread terror in whole districts.

What Ruskin has written about Corbett is also the view held by many others. But it must also be said that much of what we know about Corbett's exploits and his motives comes from his own writing about himself. The best of Corbett's adventures can be found in his books. He wrote six in all and all of them became bestsellers. His most famous was *Man-Eaters of Kumaon*, which Ruskin recalled had been made into a Hollywood film starring Sabu. But the film bombed at the box-office in spite of getting a favourable review by the noted Hollywood critic Hedda Hopper. Corbett too had been asked to give an endorsement for the film but in his usual polite way, had declined. Clearly, tigers are better looking in real life! 'One of my tiger stories too was made into a film by a brave director,' writes Ruskin. 'It featured a tiger from a local circus and also starred the noted thespian Tom Alter as the shikari...But it too failed at the box office. The tiger kept disappearing every evening back to the circus to have his dinner...Difficult to have tigers in your film. They cannot act.' While Ruskin did say that more information on the film could be had from Tom Alter, I never did get a chance to ask Tom, not even when we participated together in a programme on Corbett for the Jim Corbett Trust at the British Council in Delhi.

But let us return to *Man-Eaters of Kumaon*, and let me tell you of an incident involving the publication of this popular classic to prove that while tigers may or may not smile, they certainly do act. But we will come to the incident in good time. First, we must go back to the publishing history of *Man-Eaters of Kumaon* by Oxford University Press in 1944. It became an almost instant bestseller and has remained continuously in print, but the circumstances of its publishing were curious to say the least.

'Dear Sirs, I am writing to ask if you will undertake to publish a book for me,' stated a letter dated 15 August 1943 to the Publisher at Oxford University Press in Bombay. Not much as letters go, and set in the tones of a hopeful author seeking a publisher. The publisher could be forgiven for casting the letter into the slush pile. But something in the letter caught Roy Hawkins's eye. Hawkins—Hawk to those who knew him well—was general manager of the India office of OUP, and a publisher with a formidable reputation. Corbett had included a few of his stories from the jungle as samples of his writing. He had also stated that the proposed book would have an Introduction by Sir Maurice Hallett, then Governor of the United Provinces, and a Preface by Lord Linlithgow, the Viceroy of India. But it was the stories that interested Hawk. He read them once and he read them again. Then he had them read by his friend, an American war correspondent. The friend read the stories three times. Finally, Hawk wrote to Corbett on 4 October 1943 that he had read the stories with great interest and would like to undertake their publication. However, he would like to have more stories to select from and could

Corbett include some photographs too? In response, Corbett sent a book titled *Jungle Stories*, printed on a hand-operated press, for Hawk to make a better selection of stories.

The circumstances of the printing of *Jungle Stories* were equally interesting. In Corbett's own words: 'At [a] dinner at Government House, my hostess who had heard part of my conversation at the table, came up to me and asked if I had committed any of my jungle experiences to paper. I pleaded not guilty. She then surprised me by asking how intensely selfish it was of me for not having done so. Before leaving, the good lady had extricated a promise from me that I would write up some of my jungle experiences for the benefit of readers. For many days, I avoided the good lady but one day, I inevitably had to meet her and knowing what her first question would be, took a sheet of paper and wrote the title of a story and under it wrote Chapter One. That evening, the pleasure in the lady's eyes when I told her I had made a start so shamed me that I resolved to write up some of my jungle experiences even if no one read them. I have never kept a notebook and have never made a note in my life but there is no need to make notes, for everything I see is photographed in my memory. I took my stories to a friend who had a small hand-printing press who undertook to print it. However, his stock of type was so limited, that he could print only one page at a time and each time, the type was broken up to compose the next page. In this way, it took us four months to print 100 copies. Retaining one copy, I distributed the rest to friends. Then a concerted demand was made to publish the stories in regular book form. While in service during the war, I had prepared a manuscript copy of the book and on discharge, wrote to the Bombay branch of Oxford University Press who accepted it for publication as the *Man-Eaters of Kumaon.*'

So Hawk now had a selection of stories to choose from. But he also wanted some photographs, and if there were any included in *Jungle Stories*, these were not to his liking. He wrote to Corbett, 'You probably have other photographs which might be equally suitable for reproduction. All your tigers are dead, as they deserve to be, but if you have been able to capture some live shots, they would be interesting.' While there is no record of a written response to this from Corbett, it is believed that he replied that had the tigers been alive, *he* may not have been! But in the event, he did send Hawk more photographs, including 'Bachelor of Powalgarh', which measured 10 feet x 7 inches.

Hawk spent considerable time selecting the final stories to go into the book. He also got Corbett to revise and tighten up some of them. In a letter to Corbett dated 15 October 1943, Hawk wrote, 'The public is hard to please and—like other game—seldom gives a second chance.' Hawk also suggested that the title *Jungle Stories* was far too ordinary and proposed *Man-Eaters of Kumaon* instead. Corbett agreed, and also got the promised Introduction and Preface by Hallett and Linlithgow. *Man-Eaters of Kumaon* was finally published in 1944. Despite Hawk's general pessimism about the reading public's commitment to books when it came to actually buying them, he proposed a print-run of 4,000 copies priced at Rs 5. On the inside page Corbett inserted a message to the effect that his share from the proceeds of the sale of the book would be donated to the Dunstans Hospital in Dehradun for airmen and other soldiers blinded during the World War. OUP contributed one-fifths of the sale proceeds to Dunstans. Inspired by this, even Butterworth, the designer of the jacket cover, donated his fees to Dunstans. The fickle public was more than willing to give more than a second chance to Corbett. A thousand copies were sold in the first month in Bombay alone. When OUP began distributing the book from its offices in Madras and Calcutta, things really started moving. The initial print-run of 4,000 was a major investment given the acute shortage of paper on account of the war. The overwhelming success of the first printing and the acclaim of reviewers and readers prompted OUP to think of a second edition in 1945. But the best was yet to come.

Hawk had already sent an advance copy of the book to the OUP offices in New York soon after its publication. Now, in a letter dated 4 July 1945, he drew New York's attention to positive reviews of *Man-Eaters of Kumaon* by Associated Press and *Time*, which believed the book would be popular in the US. He also made an offer: 'England is likely to print the book and the royalty payable is 15%, if you can spare the paper for a reprint.'

The paper shortage on account of the war had affected the US too, though perhaps not as much as England and India, but the response from the New York office was positive. In a letter dated 4 August 1945, Henry Walck, Vice President of the New York office of OUP, wrote that they proposed to print an edition of 7,000 copies but proposed a break-up of royalties as follows: 10 per cent on the sale of the first 2,000 copies, 12 ½ per cent on the next 3,000 copies, 15 per cent on the balance. New York's slightly generous print-run at the time was prompted by the successful sale of extracts on an exclusive basis to the *Reader's Digest*. OUP knew that the extracts would generate wide publicity for the book. In fact, *Reader's Digest* eventually increased its extract from 6,000 to 7,000 words. Thus, the US edition was poised to launch in late 1945—when a major development forced OUP New York to completely change its plans.

This was the selection of *Man-Eaters of Kumaon* as a Book-of-the-Month by the Book Club Associates. The Book Club would print its own Book Club edition and the selection would result in an initial print-run of 250,000 copies. The Book Club had a membership of 500,000 and increased demand could even result in a print-run of 400,000 copies. There was now high excitement in the OUP offices in New York, England and India. An immediate result was that the New York office postponed its launch to April 1946 to coincide with the release of the Book Club edition and the launch had now to be upgraded to that of a major event appropriate to a book that was making such waves.

The organization of the launch for *Man-Eaters of Kumaon* became the responsibility of Virginia Carrick, the publicity director of OUP New York. Very soon Carrick realized that the launch was a 'big ticket item' and she had to pull out all the stops. As a first step, she realized, she had to get Jim Corbett to the launch. All the publicity the book had so far generated had resulted in Corbett becoming a bit of a sensation—as mysterious as he was, suddenly and unexpectedly, famous. He had admirers from the US Secretary of State to Margaret Bourke-White, the photographer who had a close connection with India, particularly with Mahatma Gandhi. Carrick chose the Hotel Pierre in Manhattan as the venue for the launch. (This iconic hotel has now been acquired by the Indian Taj group of hotels.) A stellar audience was assured for the event and all of them were eager to meet Corbett at the launch now scheduled for 4 April 1946.

Carrick approached Corbett through Hawk and between them they were able to persuade Corbett to undertake the long and potentially exhausting journey to New York. Corbett was to fly via the American Army Transport Command on a British Overseas Airways Corporation flight and he was to have a priority clearance. But in spite of the best efforts of officials in New York and London, Corbett was unable to obtain passage under the military quota. His status was that of a civilian and priority was given to military personnel demobilized and returning home in the aftermath of the war. There is no doubt that had Corbett been able to make the trip, the appearance at the launch would have only been the beginning. There would have been interviews over the radio, 'whistle-stop' tours for talks and signing sessions across the US. But it was not to be. On his part, Corbett wrote up the account of how he came to write the book and sent it to Carrick as a long cablegram via a P&O liner. In his absence, this account would have to do.

A bitterly disappointed Carrick gratefully accepted this from Corbett and decided to use it at the launch, for she knew the audience would be fascinated. But she still faced a challenge, though, as Corbett had been billed as the main draw and she had to make the audience 'feel' his presence. One of the most remarkable and eloquent appreciations of Corbett was a seven-page letter written to Carrick by Marjorie Clough in January 1946. Clough had been a member of the American Red Cross in India and excited by the news of the launch of *Man-Eaters of Kumaon*, had written to Carrick about her own meeting with Corbett. Clough had invited Corbett to speak to the Red Cross volunteers in Agra when Corbett was visiting the city to speak to the Royal Air Force. Corbett agreed, and spoke about some of his experiences in the jungle and also showed some footage of films he had taken. Clough's letter stated: 'To say that he had an audience of 300 men that evening spellbound is to say only half. We were touched by his humility in presenting his jungle films, the result of ten years of patient work in the jungles, when he forsook rifle for camera so that thousands may actually be able to see tigers in their native haunts.' Clough was so captivated with Corbett that she and a colleague spent a week with Corbett and his sister in Kaladhungi. The long letter recounted not only their adventures there but also Corbett's early life in India, his work as a contractor for the railways at Mokameh Ghat (Mokama Ghat,

Bihar) and his participation in World War I at the age of thirty-nine. He took 500 men from the Kumaon Hills to serve in a Labour Corps in France and brought back 499 safely. Carrick was so taken up by Clough's letter that she printed 2,000 copies and sent them off to the press and leading booksellers. The American Booksellers Association invited Clough to speak on Corbett, making Carrick miss Corbett even more.

But the show must go on. Carrick now attempted something that had not been done at any book launch before. She managed to get two tiger cubs from the Miami Zoo. They were to take Corbett's place as the 'guests of honour'. The cubs were twelve weeks old and came with their Austrian trainer, Captain Proske. They had to be transported by air, and finding a carrier willing to take on the 'cargo' was an uphill task. Carrick had also to arrange for insurance cover for staff and guests at the Pierre in case the cubs got too playful! The tiger cubs, perhaps conscious of the momentous occasion, put on their best act. For a start, they looked so adorable that they charmed even the hotel's banquet manager, who offered to give up his own room to the cubs in case Proske could not keep them in his. Carrick, a true publicist to the core, realized the immense value of the cubs. Just before the launch, she took Proske and the cubs to the studios of the National Broadcasting Radio to be interviewed by Mary Margaret McBride on the Women's Hour programme, at the time the biggest in the country. The interview, with a built-in phone facility from the listeners, was ostensibly a discussion between

McBride and Proske on Corbett's *Man-Eaters of Kumaon* but soon became liberally interspersed with McBride's vivid descriptions of the cubs and their antics. McBride was given to lacing her sentences with adjectives in the superlative and the cubs saw to it that their actions ensured plenty of them. Enthusiastic calls from audiences jammed the telephone lines. With this kind of build-up, Carrick knew that the launch would be an enormous success. But she had one more card to play.

Carrick decided she would get the cubs to autograph one of the copies, initially as a special gesture for Corbett, but also for other guests who might care for the cubs' signature now that they could not get that of the author. Fearing that the normal ink-stamp pad may poison the paws of the cubs, she sent for the special stamps used by meat packers to stamp their meat. When the stamps arrived, the cubs dutifully dipped their paws and put their pugmarks on the preliminary pages. With one copy kept aside for Corbett, and a couple probably for the OUP New York archives, the rest went to members of the audience lucky enough to get an autographed copy. The pugmarks were later reproduced in all subsequent editions.

Stocks of the book in New York sold out within a month and the US office had to reprint in May 1946. This, coupled with the Book Club edition sales, ensured that total sales that year were close to 490,000 copies, making *Man-Eaters of Kumaon* an all-time bestseller and Jim Corbett a household name across the world.

A PATRICIAN AMONG PUBLISHERS

RAVI DAYAL (1937-2006)

One of my early encounters with Ravi Dayal was on an afternoon in 1984, just outside the Oxford University Press office on Delhi's Ansari Road. I was working with Macmillan then and had just stepped outside the office after lunch when Ravi spotted me. The Macmillan office was 'cheek by jowl' with that of OUP's. Ravi beckoned me and as I approached, he said he had something to show me. Stepping into the OUP showroom, he pulled out a copy of Oleg Polunin and Adam Stainton's magnificent work, *Flowers of the Himalaya*, which had just been published. It had been typeset at the Aurobindo Ashram Press in Pondicherry and printed at the Indraprastha Press in Delhi. As I leafed through and looked at the wonderful colour plates, I wondered at the market and readership for the book and how many copies OUP had printed. 'We printed 750 copies,' said Ravi and seemed confident that he would be able to sell out the stock. He was even planning a reprint. 'Wow,' I said, for Ravi was clearly enthusiastic about the book. I could not contemplate Macmillan investing in a reference work of this kind and being as confident. Seeing that I was quite incredulous, Ravi introduced me to two of his senior colleagues, who also joined us at the showroom, Santosh Mookerjee, then Deputy General Manager of OUP, and Prabir Bhambal, the Branch Manager of the Delhi office. 'It's Prabir's guys who will mainly account for the sales,' Ravi said, 'apart from our other offices, of course.' I had spent enough time in publishing to know that Delhi, and the northern India market it catered for, did indeed account for the bulk of the academic and general books market and OUP excelled in such a list.

Little did I dream that one day I would hold the same charge as Prabir and would have to tap sales into that very market. While we were chatting that afternoon, I spotted an editor hurriedly coming into the office after a late lunch. Surprised and a little embarrassed that three of her bosses were milling around in the showroom, she brushed past us quickly with a hurried apology. As she turned, the heel of her shoe caught the edge of the coir matting on the showroom floor and she stumbled. She would have fallen but for the ever-gallant Prabir who steadied her. Now more embarrassed than ever, she hurried on. I knew the young editor, Kunku Saxena, as she had earlier worked with Macmillan. I actually knew her even before that, from my days at the Jawaharlal Nehru University (JNU) where she had registered for a PhD in history on study leave from her teaching stint at the Lady Shri Ram College for Women. She was Kunku Soota then, her maiden name. As Kunku hurried on, more than a little flustered, Ravi frowned, and looked at Prabir. 'We must change the carpet, Prabir,' said Ravi. 'That's great, Ravi,' I said. 'Had the same incident happened next door, the managing director there would have said, change the editor!' We all had a hearty laugh but it symbolized the difference in the working culture of the two organizations.

This was not my first acquaintance with Ravi. Sometime earlier, I had come to Delhi from Shillong as a visiting fellow at the Centre for Policy Research on lien from my teaching stint at the North-Eastern Hill University (NEHU). Keen on exploring options in publishing that would keep me in Delhi, I had approached OUP for a job. Ravi, already the general manager then, had met me but was unable to commit to an offer as he had a couple of other candidates in mind. Moreover, the salary I could expect was a little less than what I was getting already. But Ravi had kept me in mind.

In 1985, Ravi called me in to the OUP office to meet him. I guessed there was now a position that I could fill, and Ravi wanted to interview me. By then, the branch and head office in OUP had been physically separated and the latter had moved into svelte new premises at the YMCA Library Building on Jai Singh Road. The interiors had been designed by Ravi's architect friend Romi Khosla. The individual cabins looked elegant and the corridors were lined with carpets the colour of red wine. But more impressive than anything else, the office was centrally air conditioned, a truly democratic gesture at a time when air conditioners were allotted on a strict seniority basis. This, I knew, was Ravi's contribution with a budget sanction from his bosses in Oxford. (Ravi's deputy Santosh, I remember, was never comfortable with air conditioning and always felt it was against the law of nature!)

The 'interview' with Ravi was an eye-opener. It was more of a rambling chat, with Ravi taking pains to put me at ease, asking questions about university teaching, books and authors I had read and also about the state of the social sciences in the universities. Along the way, he quizzed me about the publishing process and what I thought about the market for academic books, etc. Through our conversation, he also got an idea about my standard of English. In the end, an hour had passed and I realized that Ravi had dispensed with the formality of a written test which was 'de-rigueur' for all aspiring editors. Ravi seemed satisfied with our encounter but I was still left guessing as he told me not to put in my papers at Macmillan till the Press (as OUP was popularly called) contacted me formally. I sounded Kunku who had also gone through the same process. Kunku sounded very skeptical and pessimistic. 'Ravi takes a long time to make up his mind, if at all,' she said. In her case, it had taken six months!

When a month had passed and there was no word from OUP, an intermediary offered to contact Ravi on my behalf. I was hoping this would not backfire. Fortunately, it did not. I found out that Ravi had made up his mind almost immediately and had forwarded my CV to Santosh to put in the 'nuts and bolts' and issue the formal letter of appointment. The delay was because Santosh just wanted to meet me once before issuing the letter. But soon after this, the whole thing was expedited and I met Santosh, who made me a good offer, and also informed me that the Press provided lunch to all its staff! Suddenly, Santosh was in a hurry and asked me how soon I could join. I said that I had a three-month notice period with Macmillan. Well, Santosh asked me to join as quickly as I could but also wanted me to leave Macmillan with goodwill. Which I duly did and joined OUP later in 1985, excited to work under Ravi Dayal, whose reputation as publisher was sky high. I also was to learn subsequently that *Flowers of the Himalaya* had a successful sales history, being reprinted with corrections in 1985 and again in 1986.

*

Ravi Dayal had joined the Press in 1961 after finishing his Master's degree from University College at Oxford. He was on course to do a PhD along with his friend Vinit Haksar when they heard that OUP was recruiting editors for their Bombay office in India. As a lark, perhaps, both of them appeared for the interview and Ravi was selected. Vinit went on to distinguish himself academically and his books were later published by OUP India. Soon after the interview, Ravi got to meet Roy Hawkins, the general manager of OUP in India. Hawkins, or 'Hawk' as he was more popularly known, had already acquired legendary status. Ravi was to work closely with Hawk in India till the latter retired in 1970.

Initially, Ravi worked in the OUP office at Amen Corner in London to 'learn the ropes'. In one of his recollections of those early years, Ravi mentioned that he used to leave the OUP office at 5 pm every evening. This prompted curious looks from his colleagues as he passed their desks on the way to the exit. It was then gently pointed to him that office hours were till 5.30 pm. It also amused Ravi that the initial period of apprenticeship at the London office ended with him being given a 'tropical allowance' to equip himself to work in the Bombay office.

The initial years of working under Hawk who had nurtured and developed authors like Jim Corbett, Verrier Elwin and Salim Ali were full of learning and Ravi, not given to praising anyone lightly, soon developed a respect and admiration for Hawk. But working with Hawk was also difficult, for his manner was brusque and he made it very clear that his way was the 'right way'. At least on two occasions, Ravi came close to resigning from the Press but on both occasions it was Hawk who dissuaded him. He managed to convince Ravi that he had a great future in the Press. Living in Bombay at the time was also proving to be troublesome. Ravi had initially started staying with his aunt (his father's brother's wife) at her spacious flat in New Marine Lines. His aunt, a former national women's tennis champion, had her own set of rules and regulations which Ravi found irksome and soon wanted to move out. But getting alternative accommodation was proving difficult. Moreover, Ravi had his eye on the manager's flat above Oxford House (the OUP office) in Colaba, which was then unoccupied. But a gentle request to Hawk was firmly turned down. Hawk made it clear that only expatriate managers of the OUP office in Bombay were entitled to stay there. No local could. So the flat, which in its history had even seen a manager, German in origin, interned as an 'enemy alien' during World War II, continued to remain unoccupied till Hawk appointed another expat manager. (Ravi used to muse later that as the head of OUP in India, it was his prerogative to allocate to managers a flat in which he himself had not been eligible to stay.) Ravi mended his fences with his aunt and continued to stay with her, but relations were uneasy. (I remember an occasion when my wife and I were in Ranikhet. Ravi too was there along with his wife Mala and daughter Naina, and all three came to our hotel to meet us. I told Ravi we would have been happy to call on him at his home. Ravi explained that they were staying at Himalayana, his aunt's home, and that as she was in residence at the time, it would not have been convenient to have visitors. Eventually, though, Ravi inherited Himalayana after his aunt's death.)

Ravi continued to work with Hawk in Bombay for about nine years, learning from the senior colleague and growing into an exceptional editor. Hawk was succeeded by Charles Lewis as general manager whose six-year tenure saw major reorganization in the Press, including the establishment of a branch office in Delhi and the eventual move of the head office from Bombay to Delhi. The three senior colleagues working with Charles all became assistant general managers: Neil O'Brien in Calcutta, Santosh Mookerjee (recently recruited from Orient Longman) in Delhi and Ravi Dayal, who was also chief editor. Santosh became the first manager of the newly established branch at Delhi. Charles eventually opted to go back to Oxford and he was succeeded by

Ravi as general manager in 1976 at the comparatively young age of thirty-nine.

Ravi continued to head the publishing division as well, and resolved very early not to allow the additional administrative responsibilities to come in the way of developing a fine publishing list, nurturing some fine authors and recruiting excellent editors. The list of authors, particularly in the social sciences, read like a veritable who's who in academia: Irfan Habib and Romila Thapar in history; M.N. Srinivas, Andre Beteille and Ashis Nandy in Sociology and Social Psychology; S. Gopal, who wrote masterly biographies of Jawaharlal Nehru and Sarvepalli Radhakrishnan; Ranajit Guha, whose first book was *Elementary Aspects of Peasant Insurgency in India*, and who went on to edit seven volumes of *Subaltern Studies* for OUP, now standard reference for researchers on the subject. M.N. Srinivas, who gave a new interpretation to the study of caste in India and the concept of 'Sanskritization', had the satisfaction of seeing his *The Remembered Village* reissued in the Oxford India Paperbacks series. He became a close personal friend of Ravi's and used to supply him with avocados from Bangalore after retirement.

There were other authors too who came to OUP India in Ravi's time, like K.N. Raj, Sukhamoy Chakravarty, Amit Bhaduri and Amartya Sen in economics. Amartya was to remark later that the Indian edition of his *India: Economic Development and Social Opportunities* was even more elegant than the edition produced at Oxford! In political science, we had Francine Frankel, an old

India hand from the University of Pennsylvania, and Sibnarayan Ray, who spent many years at the La Trobe University at Melbourne. Francine, in addition to her study of India's Green Revolution, edited a fine two-volume work, *Dominance and State Power in India,* along with M.S.A. Rao. Sibnarayan Ray, for long associated with M.N. Roy's Radical Humanist organization and the People's Union for Civil Liberties (PUCL), went on to edit a multi-volume series, *The Selected Works of M.N. Roy*, which remains an invaluable reference for the history and politics of the first half of the 20th century.

The list in literature and cultural studies included the legendary A.K. Ramanujan, AKR, then Colvin Professor of Languages and Civilization at Chicago. He too became a close friend of Ravi's, though his poetry had been originally published by OUP New York. Ravi used to refer to him as 'Raman' and was distraught when AKR died so tragically in what should have been a routine appendicitis operation.

Ravi had a great love for poetry, and among the poets he published in the celebrated 'Three Crowns' series were such giants of Indian English poetry as Keki Daruwalla, Nissim Ezekiel, Gieve Patel and Imtiaz Dharker, among others. While consolidating the Ornithology and Wildlife series, Ravi published the *Encyclopedia of Indian Natural History* in collaboration with the Bombay Natural History Society (BNHS) edited by Roy Hawkins, possibly the last work edited by Hawk; and Salim Ali's autobiography, *The Fall of a Sparrow*.

Ravi's equation with almost every author he published

serves as an example of what an ideal author-publisher relationship should be—one of mutual respect, above everything else. Very often the relationship grew into deep personal bonding. Ravi was not one to show his emotions in public, but he cared deeply for his authors and was very keen that they continue to give their best work to the Press. Sometimes Ravi's own reading and often the anonymous external reader's report would suggest revision; in every such case, Ravi would write to the author enclosing the reader's report, explaining why the changes were necessary, and suggesting how these could be made.

But if a manuscript or proposal was not up to the mark, Ravi had no hesitation at all in saying no. The historian and biographer Ram Guha has written that Ravi did not take a walk in Lodhi Gardens, so near his home, to avoid encountering the many authors he had rejected. But Ravi took care to draft the letter turning down a manuscript in such a manner that it preserved the author's self-respect and dignity. We were all encouraged to word our rejection letters very carefully, saying that our turning down the manuscript was in no way a reflection on its scholarship and we wished the author every success with another publisher. And very often, the author did find acceptance with another publisher.

Yet, Ravi could also quiz an editor thoroughly about why a particular manuscript was turned down. I remember once Ravi gave me a manuscript by C.V. Narasimhan who had had a distinguished career as Under Secretary General for the United Nations. I read it and found it rather verbose and too much in the first person singular, and full of self-praise. I had no hesitation in recommending that we turn it down, but Ravi would have none of it. 'CVN was quite a knowledgeable guy. My brother Viru worked in the UN with him. How can you say no?' he asked. Viru was Ravi's brother Virendra Dayal, who had himself had a distinguished career in the UN as the 'chef-de-cabinet' to the Secretary General. I made a fair offer to Ravi. If he could read up to fifty pages and it still held his interest, well, I would look at the manuscript again. Ravi could not go beyond ten pages and the manuscript was rejected.

It wasn't only editors who were subjected to such scrutiny. An author like B.R. Nanda, the eminent historian and biographer and the first director of the Nehru Memorial Museum and Library, was once quizzed rather strenuously on his manuscript, yet Ravi was the first to acknowledge publicly that Nanda had defended himself admirably. Ravi could be gracious to first-time authors too. A young historian once wrote to him to say how excited she was to have her first work published by OUP, even though for Ravi it probably was routine. She also added that the Press had done a fine job and in particular, her editor. Ravi took pains to reply. He thanked her for her appreciation and said he too was proud of her work and happy that the Press had published it, and promised to convey her sentiments to all his colleagues.

Ravi was almost spartan both in his living and in his habits. Lean and spare in his trademark kurta and trousers, his concession to winter was a pullover or a waistcoat.

His only indulgence was the beedi that he smoked—a strong statement of individuality, and also, perhaps, a kind of political signalling: beedis over cigarettes, Indian-made whiskey over Scotch. As long as he was on Ansari Road, Daryaganj, Ravi had a regular supply of beedis from a single vendor. When the office shifted to Jai Singh Road, he got his supplies from elsewhere.

In the office, Ravi followed an 'open door' policy and never closed the door to his room. As he did not, no one else in the office could either. In theory, it meant one could walk into his office to discuss an issue at any time. If he was busy or was on a call, he stopped you with a look. Though he had a secretary, there was no need to fix an appointment. Visitors, of course, came by appointment.

Ravi was democratic in other ways too. The Jai Singh Road office was supposed to be centrally air-conditioned with a twenty-tonne air-conditioning plant. But it never ran, simply because the YMCA Library building did not have the required power. It did not have the power because it had not yet been allotted the sanctioned load, and it did not have the load because it did not have a completion certificate. A veritable conundrum if ever there was one. Someone had goofed, big time. OUP had shifted its office on the basis of a promise from the owners of the building that they would get the requisite power. The European Economic Commission (EEC) Delegation on the other hand, co-tenants of the fifth and fourth floors of the same building, had not accepted a mere promise. They had made power supply a requisite condition of their lease and secured the necessary power. Now, having spared this power, the building had no surplus to run a twenty-tonne plant. The other tenants, like the Indira Gandhi National Open University (IGNOU) and the UNICEF Greetings Cards division ran a few window air conditioners in their offices and managed. This option was offered to Ravi too. He simply refused to have an air-conditioner in his room while the rest of the office sweated in the terrible heat.

That particular summer in 1986, the second for the staff at the Jai Singh Road office, was particularly severe. Even the visiting managers from the other branch offices had their meetings in the air-conditioned conference room of the YMCA Tourist Hostel next door. This was the proverbial last straw. A special petition drawn up by the editors and signed by all staff members was submitted to Santosh, saying it was impossible to work under these conditions. It was not that people were used to air-conditioning and could not work without it. But the office interiors, with false ceilings and extensive lighting, were designed specifically for an air-conditioned work place. The only time anyone remembered the air-conditioning working was the one time that power from the EEC office had been diverted on a closed day, Saturday, to test the machines. It had been a few hours of heaven; every summer day since had been near hell. Something had to be done, and urgently. Previous attempts with the YMCA and the New Delhi Municipal Corporation (NDMC) had all failed. I then initiated efforts in contacting some bureaucrats I knew in the Delhi government. Power for running an air-conditioning plant, even one as small as ours, had to be sanctioned by the Lieutenant Governor.

This was done and we had approval from the Power Secretary. But the NDMC had dug in its heels and wanted a completion certificate and for this, a 'no objection' from the Delhi Fire Service was required. S.K. Dheri, who served for long as the chief of the Delhi fire service, obliged and sent a team, which after an inspection and the installation of additional fire extinguishers, issued the 'no objection'. After this, we obtained the completion certificate from the NDMC for only our portion of the premises. Now the feasibility and costings of a separate power cable connection from the Mandir Marg sub-station was done and after approval and payment, the connection was laid and energized.

Finally, we had the power to run the air-conditioning. It had only taken three months. Ravi acknowledged the effort. In a write-up in *The Record*, the annual newsletter with reports from all the international offices of OUP, Ravi decided to use a sporting analogy. It was the season of the 1986 Football World Cup. He wrote, '...the initial efforts to resolve the air-conditioning imbroglio were by Santosh Mookerjee and Rukun Advani. But from the quarter-finals stage onwards, Sridhar Balan played a heroic Maradona-like role against the fierce opposition mounted by the power department, the fire service and the municipality and scored goals every time. Luckily, Balan was spared having to confront the garbage cleaning services of the NDMC. At last we got the power to run our air-conditioning, not in time to ward off our June temperatures but certainly to cope with the August humidity. Our grateful thanks to him.' The Record did the rounds. For some time, Sir Roger Elliott, the Wykeham Professor of Physics at Oxford and chairman of the OUP finance committee and later the chief executive of OUP, referred to me as the 'spin doctor' on his visits to India.

Ravi's belief that there should be 'equal' facilities for all manifested itself in other areas as well. OUP shared the first-floor premises of the YMCA Library building with the IGNOU office in the opposite wing. Among other things, the washrooms too were common. One day, we had a request from the YMCA that the vice chancellor of IGNOU wanted an 'en-suite' washroom to his office. He would not share, not even with his own staff. Therefore, one of the WC cubicles would be sealed and opened up from his office room exclusively for his personal use. As we shared the facilities, the YMCA had to clear permission with us. As the 'spin doctor', I was approached and I asked them to refer the matter to Santosh. Santosh was inclined to agree. But Ravi's approval had to be sought. Ravi took a dim view of privileges that government officers and heads of public institutions enjoyed and one of them he knew was the prized 'en-suite' washroom. He told me, 'Let the vice chancellor list in detail all the ailments he suffers from with a doctor's certificate as to why he needs attached facilities. I will then take a call.' The vice chancellor was too embarrassed by this and the matter was not pursued further. Later, IGNOU shifted its office to a residential building in south Delhi where the worthy presumably got his prized 'en-suite' bathroom! Eventually, one of Ravi's successors at OUP converted the cubicle into a personal loo!

If one could walk into Ravi's office room at any time, it also meant the reverse was equally true. I remember two instances when Ravi trundled up at lunchtime, plate in hand, to discuss something. Lunch was served in the pantry, the office did not boast of a kitchen, and Ravi lined up with the rest of us and helped himself. One day he walked into my room and suddenly asked, 'Why do you think George should release M.N. Roy?' I was editing the first volume of *The Selected Works of*

M.N. Roy and it was almost ready to go to press. The 'George' Ravi was referring to was George Richardson, who had taught Economics at Oxford and was the chief executive and secretary to the delegates of OUP. George was scheduled to visit Delhi in March, a couple of months away, and it had been decided that he would release the

M.N. Roy volume at a function at the Claridges Hotel. It had all been fixed and now suddenly Ravi popped this question. It was he who had accepted the manuscript for publication in the first place! It suddenly dawned on me that Ravi was composing a telex message (that was the form of communication then) to George and wanted some points on Roy from me. It may also have been a way to test how much I had absorbed of the subject I was editing. I quickly summed up some features of Roy's life, his participation in the Comintern and his important intervention in the form of a supplement to Lenin's thesis on the national and colonial question. I also spoke about Roy's subsequent disillusionment with communism and Stalin's excesses, and his choice of radical humanism. I summed up with a bit about Roy's patriotism and his desire to see India free from colonial rule. It seemed to do the trick. Later, while releasing the book, George mentioned that he had been prejudiced against M.N. Roy for he carried a framed picture of Stalin on his mantlepiece. It was only while perusing the book that he had learned that Roy had been a humanist at heart and was deeply disturbed by Stalin's progroms in Russia.

Ravi was not a publisher with just an academic mind; he had a wide range of other interests too. These ranged from music, dance and theatre to films, sports and of course nature and wildlife. He had a fine feel for poetry as well. The second instance I remember of him walking up to me and other colleagues was also at lunchtime. He came into the room where a few of us had gathered for the office lunch, and asked, 'Have you all heard of this guy, Vikram Seth?' We confessed we hadn't. OUP was a distributor for Faber & Faber them and Ravi had received two advance copies of Faber's *The Golden Gate* from England. 'It's something new, a novel in verse, very similar to Onegin,' said Ravi and proceeded to recite a few lines. We were interested and I suggested that Ravi bring a copy of the book and read from it. Ravi duly did so and the effect was electrifying, for Ravi read poetry beautifully. We immediately resolved to import 500 copies from Faber and they sold out quickly. We then secured permission from Faber to reprint the book twice. Later, we also published Vikram's *The Humble Administrator's Garden*, before Vikram was wooed by Penguin and switched allegiance, but he never forgot OUP. Years later, after he had achieved fame and success, I met him and his brother Shantum at Penguin's launch of *Two Lives*. As soon as he saw me, Vikram nudged Shantum and said, 'You know, they published me first in India.'

*

Towards the end of 1986, Ravi dropped a bombshell. He announced his premature retirement from the Press. It caught everyone by surprise, as the head of OUP in India was one of the most prestigious publishing jobs to be had, and also intellectually satisfying. Moreover, Ravi had spent just ten years in the job and was still months short of fifty. The stipulated age of retirement in the Press was sixty. In retrospect, some felt that Ravi's speech at the international sales conference in 1986 to managers from all over the world perhaps held a hint that he might not be around for too long. But for most, to paraphrase the famous poem by Oliver Goldsmith on the village schoolmaster, it was a case of '[a]nd still they gazed and still the wonder grew'. We couldn't get our head around the fact that Ravi could throw away a job so prestigious; a job so perfect for him and one that few could do as well as him.

But once Ravi had made up his mind, there was no stopping him. He announced his decision formally to a shocked Santosh at Frankfurt where they had gone to attend the international book fair in October 1986. India was a guest of honour at the Fair. Santosh was further shocked when Ravi announced that he would like him, Santosh, to succeed him. Later, Ravi confided that Santosh was so bewildered by the turn of events, that while Ravi strode confidently from the hotel to the fair grounds, Santosh followed behind 'like a shy, demure Indian bride, eyes downcast'. Ravi also announced his intention of going to Oxford from Frankfurt before returning to Delhi. He wanted to inform Oxford of his intention, but more importantly, get acceptance of Santosh as his successor. This was crucial as Santosh had already turned sixty in 1986 and was in line for retirement as per the OUP policy. Ravi duly went to Oxford and announced his surprise move to an incredulous Roger Boning, the director of the international division and Ravi's immediate reporting head. Roger was even more surprised when Ravi proposed that Santosh should succeed him. Properly speaking, Ravi could only make a suggestion, as Oxford was the appointing authority. In any case, Roger had to consult George Richardson in the matter. But such was Ravi's stature that the suggestion was accepted. But Roger, in turn, managed to extract a commitment from Ravi that he would serve out a full six months' notice period and be available for consultation later, if required. Ravi agreed.

Farewell functions for Ravi were held in both the Jai Singh and Ansari Road offices. At the former, both Khushwant Singh (Ravi's father-in-law) and the diplomat Rajeshwar Dayal (Ravi's uncle) were present. In a somewhat emotionally charged atmosphere at Daryaganj, my colleague Rukun Advani remarked that there would be two eras in the history of OUP India: BC—Before Charles (referring to Charles Lewis, Ravi's predecessor), and AD—After Dayal. Even Rukun could not have guessed how prescient his remarks would prove. Ravi's exit was a turning point in the history of the Press, and though the Press was stable and continued to grow in both Santosh's and his successor Neil O'Brien's times, irrevocable changes in its working culture were already set in motion.

Ravi continued to drop in to the office as a consultant till his own imprint, Ravi Dayal Publisher, stabilized. It was not his intention to set up a big publishing company but to publish a select list, including some fiction. Numbering Amitav Ghosh, C.S. Jhabvala and Jayant Narlikar (with a science fiction book) among its authors, Ravi's list acquired distinction and he approached Orient Longman for distribution, which was gladly accepted.

In 2006, Ravi succumbed to lung cancer. His lungs had been compromised on account of his smoking. Admitted to hospital, his frail constitution did not survive surgery. Condoling with a sorrowful Mala and Naina at their home in Sujan Singh Park (I had been away from Delhi on the day Ravi died), I noticed that Naina had removed all the ashtrays from the living room. They were a stark reminder perhaps of a habit that eventually took away her beloved father. But Ravi had refused to be diminished by the dreaded illness. He remained the consummate editor-publisher and a perfectionist to the last. Even from hospital his long-distance conversation with Amitav Ghosh was on the origin and spelling of the Hindustani word 'gusalkhana' (bath-house).

Sometime later, the India International Centre (IIC) organized a memorial meeting for Ravi, chaired by the scholar, writer and former Maharaja of Jammu-Kashmir, Dr Karan Singh. I was invited to speak along with Keki Daruwalla, Tejeshwar Singh and Ashis Nandy. Very fine tributes were paid to Ravi in a packed hall with some former colleagues attending, but strangely no one from the current OUP office. It was left to Ashis to sum up Ravi's contribution. He said in building up one of the finest lists in scholarship pertaining to South Asia, Ravi offered a viable alternative to researchers and scholars to publish their work in India instead of having to look overseas.

But it was Karan Singh who had the last word. He recalled that he had submitted his autobiography to be published by OUP. In it, Singh had mentioned that on one of his travels abroad, he had the good fortune to meet the famous Dr Helen Keller. At the meeting, Keller, deaf and blind, summoned Singh to come closer to her. When he approached, she took her hand and ran it lightly across his face and remarked, 'Handsome.' Singh was naturally happy to put this compliment from a beautiful and gracious lady into his autobiography. Editing the manuscript, Ravi had taken his red pencil and scored the line out. In the margin he had written, 'Presumptuous.' In spite of his wishes, Singh could not get the line reinstated. I had occasion to write later to a slightly disconsolate Singh. I said the consensus in the IIC that day was not that Helen Keller was wrong, she was indeed quite right, but that Ravi Dayal was probably right; Keller's remark should probably not appear in a book written by the handsome man himself! And it is, again, a testament to the respect and affection Ravi commanded that Karan Singh accepted Ravi's decision and could even joke about it, at his own expense, in public.

THE BOOKSELLER OF HAZRATGANJ

RAM ADVANI (1920-2016)

Even a casual visitor to the city of Lucknow could not miss it. Driving down main Hazratganj, no matter which side of the road you were on, it was impossible to miss two long vertical signboards in red which said in bold letters: 'Books'. As you reached nearer the Mayfair building which had once housed the iconic Mayfair cinema theatre and Kwality restaurant, you found yourself at the shop of Ram Advani Bookseller. This was no ordinary bookshop. Nor was its proprietor Ram Advani, who more often than not could be glimpsed sitting at his desk in his signature Lukhnavi white churidar and kurta.

Quite some years ago, the academic and historian Alice Thorner, who along with her brilliant husband Daniel Thorner had published the pathbreaking *Land and Labour in South Asia*, met me over dinner on one of her trips to Delhi. Alice and Daniel had bought a house at Guy La Brosse in Paris after they moved to France from the US. The couple had spent many happy years in the house, and after Daniel's death, Alice had continued to live there alone. 'I fear I have lived for too long in Guy La Brosse,' Alice told me. 'Now I along with my house have become a monument, a must-do sight for visitors to Paris!' This, perhaps, applied even more to Ram Advani in the historic city of Lucknow. But casual visitors would not be interested in Ram Advani or his bookshop, nor he in them. For those interested in books, however, a visit to Ram Advani's bookshop was to be savoured. One came away with a deep sense of satisfaction at having had a literary encounter of the highest quality. For those of us in the publishing profession whose job it was to call on Ram to ensure that the order form was filled and we got due visibility for our books, calling on Ram was one of our more pleasant tasks. Ram was particular about the books he stocked and displayed in the showroom. He mostly stocked academic and scholarly books, along with books written for a general audience by academics. He had the best books on various aspects of Indian history and, of course, one of the most comprehensive lists on Lucknow and its rich and fascinating history.

Naturally, then, Ram's bookshop was a compulsory stop for most local academics in the social sciences, as it was for visiting academics from the rest of India and other parts of the world who specialized in subjects particular to the region. He was a vast storehouse of information and foreign academics were most grateful for his insights and references that they might look into. More useful than the references were the conversations with Ram himself, at the end of which visiting academics would sign copies of their books that were in stock with Ram. This is how Ram came to possess signed copies of books by P.J.O. Taylor, Rosie Llewelyn-Jones, Peter

Reeves and Gail Minault, among others. I remember having Ram with us at the inauguration of the OUP office-cum-showroom at Mahanagar in Lucknow along with Violette Graff, whose book *Lucknow: Memories of a City* we had published. The inauguration was by Ashok Priyadarshi, the District Magistrate of Lucknow, a rare DM with a genuine and abiding love of books and a self-confessed Ram Advani fan.

Over the years, a wonderful friendship developed between Ram and me. In 1995, Ram had completed 50 years in the book trade and since it also marked a 50-year relationship with OUP, a relationship that began in 1945, we organized a special exhibition of books in Ram's honour. But we were 'beaten to the draw' by Penguin, who organized a similar exhibition. This was due to the enterprise and initiative shown by their marketing head, Zamir Ansari, a remarkable books person and a good friend. Penguin didn't quite have the kind of books back then that Ram liked, but they had started to broaden their publishing list to include some scholarly non-fiction too. S. Gopal's *Anatomy of a Confrontation* would be published a year later, along with books by Bimal Jalan and Amit Bhaduri. Romila Thapar's *History of India*, of course, was already on Penguin's list, and a perennial bestseller. Zamir realized that he needed a trade outlet for this list, and who better than Ram Advani? Indeed. And Ram was happy to stock some of the Penguin list along with titles of OUP and Sage.

Ram was a regular visitor to the then bi-annual World Book Fair in Delhi. In those days the forenoon hours were reserved for visitors from the trade. Ram used to visit almost all the academic publishers' stalls personally and make his selections. He would also give his frank opinion to publishers on the nature of their lists and publishing policy. Once, the international sales manager of Macmillan UK was visiting and happened to be in the Macmillan stall when Ram visited. The poor fellow got an earful about all that was wrong with his company. He was a changed man after that!

I can't imagine too many other booksellers being as passionate about books or half as forthright about the state of affairs in publishing. It came from years of experience, a formidable intellect and also family history. Ram's father, Cherumal Advani, had moved to Lucknow from Karachi in the 1920s and opened a bookshop, the Lucknow Bookstall. But it turned out to be a bad business decision. Lucknow Bookstall was shut down and Cherumal decided to invest in the newly built Mayfair Cinema Theatre instead. However, this was not the end of the family's connection with bookselling. In the 1940s, Ram's maternal uncles founded the well-known bookshop J. Ray & Sons in Lahore, with branches in Rawalpindi, Peshawar and Murree. In 1944, after getting a degree from Lucknow University, and spending three years as bursar secretary and coach of the cricket team at Bishop Cotton School in Shimla, Ram joined the family business in Lahore. But just before Partition, he was forced to move to Shimla, where he set up a branch of J. Ray & Sons for his uncles. Those were troubled times and books were not the greatest priority. But Ram saw a firm future for the book business. As did his uncles, who asked him to move back to his home city and start a bookshop there. The shop opened in a corner of Lucknow's Gandhi Bhandar in 1948, where it continued for some years, patronized, because of the location, by the likes of Nehru, Acharya and Sucheta Kripalani, Feroze Gandhi and Radhakamal Mukerjee. It was a dream beginning, but Ram's uncles had suffered enormous losses in the chaos of Partition and acquiring stock from foreign publishers was becoming increasingly difficult. Ram, however, was determined to make a success of the business. In 1952, he was able to buy out the shop from his uncles, and renamed it 'Ram Advani—Bookseller'. For the next 64 years, it was one of the most charming and welcoming landmarks—indeed, monuments—of the great city of nawabi culture and refinement.

In October 2015, I checked my mobile phone to find that I had received a missed call from someone's landline. I had moved on from OUP and was working

with Ratna Sagar then. My colleagues and I had been in our annual product briefing meetings the whole day, and I had not been able to look at my phone. On checking my phone that evening, I saw a call from a number I did not recognize, with the prefix code 0522. I realized this was a Lucknow code and was puzzled, as my entire Lucknow sales team was in Delhi and I had just spoken to them. In any case, why would they call from a landline? I was intrigued and called the number only to find Ram at the other end. I was not very familiar with the shop's landline as my appointments in Lucknow were mostly fixed by my office and I would just drop in to see Ram at the appointed hour. Anyway, Ram mentioned that it had been a long time since I had last visited Lucknow and when was I coming to meet him? He also mentioned that I was one of his oldest friends and it would be a pleasure to see me. I protested that I was a friend, certainly, but surely not his 'oldest' friend! Ram ignored my protest and repeated that I was one of his oldest friends and that he would like to meet me and I should come. That was that and I promised I would plan a trip to Lucknow soon. I had met Ram in Lucknow a little after his wonderful and elegant wife Darshi had passed away and I knew that this had shaken him. Moreover, he had had a fall recently and this had made him a little unsteady on his feet. Sadly, my frequent tours to other parts of the country kept me busy and I was simply unable to make the trip. To my everlasting regret, Ram passed away in 2016 before I could see him.

My other great regret has been not being able to

record Ram's recollections and reminiscences over his many years in the trade. I mentioned this to him once at our meeting at the Lucknow Golf Club one evening. Ram asked me why I would want to do this. I said with a view to publishing it. Ram guffawed and just brushed it aside by saying who on earth would want to read about his life? But I was serious, I said, because apart from his own life, the reminiscences would be an important addition to our history of publishing in India. But Ram changed the topic. 'You know, I am now the oldest member of the Lucknow Golf Club,' he said, his eyes sparkling. He recalled the time when he had first become a member. 'In 1948, some eight members came together and collected a princely sum of rupees five each from some of us. We filled out some forms. My form was duly proposed and seconded, and hey presto, I was a member of the Lucknow Golf Club!' Of course, golf had been introduced in Lucknow at the turn of the nineteenth century for the British officers and for the army. It was a part of the United Services Club. There is still no precise date as to when the fairways were laid out at the present course but from the mid-1950s, Ram played a major role, along with other veteran members, in the club acquiring its present status.

The older members passed on in due course, including Ram's co-signatories on the membership form, and Ram soon found that he was the oldest member, much like Wodehouse's oldest member of the golf club in his inimitable books *The Clicking of Cuthbert* and in *The Heart of a Goof*. Almost all of Wodehouse's golf stories are related by the oldest member, mostly to a younger member. The oldest member's golfing days were over but once he started on his stories, he could not be stopped. But Ram's golfing days were far from over. Till his mid-seventies, he could still play a full 18-round hole of golf and thereafter, he would play the half-course. He built up a formidable reputation as a player and had an enviable handicap in single digits. Though he favoured playing at the Army course in the cantonment later, he continued to visit the Lucknow Golf Club.

Unlike Wodehouse's oldest member, Ram did not relate too many golf stories to me. But he did tell me an interesting anecdote about Martinpurva, the village which bordered the golf course. It was named after the French adventurer Claude Martin who founded the La Martiniere schools in Lucknow, Calcutta and Lyons. In fact, Martin's residence, La Constantia, could be seen from the golf course. Ram said such close proximity to the golf course restricted the career choices for the young lads of Martinpurva. 'They either became caddies or crooks.' Ram then mentioned some of the more famous caddies who had 'carried' for him and became good golfers. But he did not mention any of those who had taken to the latter profession!

If publishing can be described as 'a gentleman's profession', then bookselling is equally so. Moved by a passionate commitment and a deep love for books, Ram developed the promotion of books into a fine art. He was knowledgeable about almost all the books he carried and treated them with reverence and respect. A books was not merely a 'product' to him but the result of an author's hard work in partnership with a publisher who would give it final shape. In addition to books, Ram was one of the few booksellers who kept a stock of *Biblio: A Review of Books*. Founded by Dileep Padgaonkar, Arvind Das and Darryl D'Monte with Sham Lal as Editor-Emeritus, *Biblio* had developed into an excellent review journal. I had contributed a number of review articles to it over the years and had also become a member of its board of trustees. The publishing industry supported it in the form of advertisements but it had its financial constraints. I remember Sham Lal once telling me, 'Dileep has produced a fine journal but it always seems to be in the ICU!' Simply put, *Biblio* required better promotion for only increased sales would help it emerge from the red. For his part, Ram played a major role in increasing the visibility of *Biblio* in Lucknow and also advertised that most of the books reviewed in the journal were great books and available in his shop.

Meeting Ram at the shop was always a memorable experience. He was a connoisseur of western classical instrumental music and its soft strains would waft through the speakers at all times of the day. He had created a small mezzanine floor for his office, and if you were a close friend, you were invited to relax there with a cup of Lopchu tea brewed personally by him. Sometimes, he would order tea from the Kwality restaurant next door. As age took its toll, Ram confined himself to the ground-floor showroom and tea would be served there. After he gave up driving, Ram would hire a cycle-rickshaw to take him home for lunch and an afternoon nap. In the evening, he was back at the shop. In case one was lucky to be invited for a drink at his home in Lawrence Terrace, presided over by Darshi, who was the perfect hostess, one was in for a great evening. The highlight of the evening was when Ram asked you to sign the very distinguished 'Visitor's Book' sitting on a comfortable leather recliner. This was a singular privilege and over the years, the book came to carry some very great names and in its own way, was a record of visitors to Ram's bookshop.

Ram may verily have been the 'last Sindhi in a rickshaw' in Lucknow much like the proverbial 'last Parsi in a tonga' in Bombay—a charming, cultured book-lover in a charming, cultured city. But like his community brethren, he was also a shrewd businessman. Most publishers would supply books to Ram at the agreed discount and credit period which could vary between 90 and 120 days from the date of the invoice. Knowing that the type of books he carried sold over a longer period of time, Ram would discount the month in which the supplies were made and reckon the credit period as starting from the next month. In this way, he enjoyed a little extra credit period. But he would always pay promptly when it was due by *his* 'calculation'. Well, not always promptly, and sometimes on my visit I would be asked by my office to gently remind him. Ram would always disarm me by saying, 'You surely aren't going to ask me for payment?' with a twinkle in his eye. But our meeting would invariably go off well and I would ask the office to collect the cheque from Ram the next day, as he would be in a good mood! Ram valued relationships and he felt there was really no substitute to conversations about books and authors with old friends.

But possibly the greatest joy for Ram, and perhaps the acid test for a true bookseller, was to procure a book for a customer not easily available in a shop even in the big metropolises like Delhi, Bombay and Calcutta. Ram would go to great lengths to procure the book, even if it was only to be found abroad. He would add on the freight charges to the cost of the book but when it arrived, one could not say whose joy was greater, the customer's or Ram's! Customers were always important to him. Even during the exhibition held in his honour to mark his 50 years in the book trade, he arrived late and apologized that he had been attending to the Nawab of Mahmudabad, an old friend, who had dropped in hoping to find some good books to read. Book buyers are notoriously fickle creatures, they need to be cajoled and sometimes even seduced by the allure of a good bargain before they can be persuaded to buy. Moreover, going to a bookshop is always a subjective experience. For the buyer to make a repeat visit, the first visit has to be good. The number of repeat customers at Ram's bookshop not only testified to his skills as a bookseller but also to the respect and confidence customers reposed in him. It was the experience in Ram's bookshop that they craved and even in later years, as the facade of Hazratganj began to change and, more particularly, the Mayfair Arcade changed, with parking becoming a major problem, the regulars were always there.

Once, in a philosophical mood, Ram remarked that a lifetime in the book trade had given him all the satisfaction and contentment he could have hoped for, and the financial returns too had been adequate, if not great. He firmly believed in the future of the printed book but his one regret was that young people were not reading as much as they used to and he wanted more people to take up a career in the book trade. Still, it must have given him great satisfaction that both his children, Rukun and Radhika, developed a great love for books and for reading, with Rukun carving out his own career as a distinct publisher with a quality list.

Today, the Lucknow Golf Club holds an annual golf tournament in memory of Ram Advani. It's time the publishing industry also did something to preserve his legacy, now that Ram's bookshop has gone the way of so many old landmarks in Lucknow.

A SHOWROOM WHERE BOOKS MATTERED

In 1984, the OUP head office was divided. The head office, which had been moved from Bombay to Delhi and had been functioning from the same premises as the branch, on Delhi's Ansari Road, since 1972, was set to move again. This was a plan strategized by Bill Mitchell, then head of the international division at OUP, Oxford. A year earlier, various alternative premises for the head office had been considered, till half a floor, about 4,000 square feet, in the newly-built YMCA Library on Jai Singh Road in the heart of downtown New Delhi was finalized. Ravi Dayal, the head of OUP India at the time, got his friend, the architect Romi Khosla, to design the interiors and a spanking new office emerged with carpeting in the corridors and central air-conditioning. It was unlike anything the lesser mortals working in publishing had ever seen. For a few weeks after the head office staff had moved in, their colleagues from the branch office, still on Ansari Road, would drop in on some pretext or the other just to see the new office. For some time, the OUP head office attracted as many footfalls as the Jantar Mantar monument, a stone's throw away. It was all very upmarket and elegant. Never mind that the air-conditioning wasn't set in operation for a full year, as has been explained earlier in the book.

The rationale for the move was simple. The functions of the head office were different to those of the branch office. Apart from finance, the head office combined editorial, design and production functions and it would be easier for authors to drop in for discussions, as Ansari Road was getting increasingly crowded. But there was a price that the head office staff had to pay for the move and this was that it physically separated them from books. This may sound strange, for the editors maintained all the references that they would require for their functioning in their rooms. *The Chicago Manual of Style*, Judith Butcher's *Copy-Editing*, *Hart's Rules* and dictionaries, notably *The Oxford Advanced Learner's Dictionary*, were on their shelves. Moreover, the editors also had advance copies of all the books they had edited as manuscripts. So what books would they be separated from?

The answer lay in the location of the OUP showroom, which remained on Ansari Road. It was no ordinary showroom; there was no other quite like it. In addition to all the books the India office produced, it had a whole host of titles imported from OUP, Oxford and OUP, New York, apart from other OUP offices worldwide. Moreover, OUP represented the prestigious literary imprint Faber & Faber, along with university presses like Harvard, Stanford and Princeton and Blackwell Science. For those interested in books and reading, it was a veritable feast for the eyes.

Ravi Dayal did his best to remedy the situation. He had his own room on Jai Singh Road designed with adequate shelving for books. He also stocked the shelves in the reception area and in a part of the corridor with some of the imported list. Ravi wanted to give the impression that this was a publisher's office where books mattered. When I joined the OUP head office just a year after its shift, I would discover gems like Robert Capa's *Photographs*, Jane Goodall's book on chimpanzees, T.S. Eliot's *The Wasteland* and even a book on Willa Cather, the relatively unknown author from Nebraska, on whom an aunt of mine was to do her PhD! Even Francis Younghusband's lesser known work, *The Heart of a Continent*, was there, along with Lord Birkenhead's *Kipling*. But despite such efforts, it was a losing task. The head office staff had to commute to the showroom if they wanted to see the full range of books, and Ravi himself went there on Saturday mornings, when the rest of the OUP offices were closed.

There is a passage in Upamanyu Chatterjee's *English, August* where the protagonist, Agastya Sen, while driving past the showrooms of OUP and Macmillan, which were next to each other on Ansari Road, wonders who on earth would ever read the dusty tomes on display in the showroom windows. A pity that he didn't step in. For the OUP showroom, at least, had always attracted a steady stream of people. These were mostly academics, researchers and students. OUP had established the practice of giving a discount to all its authors, not only on their own books but also on whatever else they wanted to buy. Sometimes non-OUP academics would get their colleagues to buy books on their behalf to avail of the discount. OUP also had an attractive discount for office staff, in the hope of encouraging them to read. This would result in some decent over the counter sales—the authors had the facility of getting the cost of their purchases deducted from their royalty statements, but the rest paid cash. I emphasize this because the bulk of the books in the trade are sold to distributors on a credit basis, with statements being made up at the end of their credit periods. Even presuming these payments are received on time (which they rarely are), it is not a system that favours publishers. Cash sales, therefore, are like answered prayers!

The importance of the showroom on Ansari Road was seen early by the OUP management both at the head office and the branch office. Periodic attempts had been made in the past to refurbish and renovate the showroom, given the clientele it attracted. In the era before computerization, authors like Romila Thapar, Andre Beteille and Ashis Nandy would go down to the trade section in the basement of the branch office to get their billing done. There was really no alternative. There was no retail bookshop in the city that carried a good number of the OUP titles—or titles by any other academic publisher, for that matter—for selection by individual customers. Unlike the exclusive OUP bookshop on High Street in Oxford and the OUP/Zwemmer bookshop at Charing Cross in London, OUP India had no bookshop of its own. It sold mostly to libraries and institutions. Thus, the OUP showroom became a focal point for individuals to select books. Also, individual academics and researchers had contingency grants for their projects and this money had to be spent on the purchase of books.

The OUP showroom got a thorough refurbishing when Prabir Bhambal was the branch manager. Emboldened by the shift of the head office and seeing the impressive outfitting there, Prabir decided that the showroom needed a thorough overhaul. Emulating Ravi, he too appointed an architect to redesign the showroom and along with it, his own office and that of Manzar Khan, the assistant manager. He approved the design and estimates and got in air-conditioning too. His room and that of Manzar's sported new carpets and there were new cupboards and shelves as well. The showroom acquired a more comfortable and cheerful ambience and Prabir was satisfied that the entire branch office now looked like the branch office with the largest business turnover among all the others should. Unfortunately, Prabir got transferred to the head office soon thereafter. He always regretted that he did not stay long enough to enjoy the office he had transformed! Manzar succeeded him, and for a while, performed the dual functions of managing the branch as well as overall marketing. He then had to finally move over to the head office, too, and I became the branch head, on transfer from the head office. I would insist that the sales staff spend time in the evenings, after their sales calls, in the showroom. It was the best way to get to know the books and the stocks we carried. This would always come in handy. I would repeat Neil O'Brien's stock question to all potential sales recruits: 'You are asked to visit a new retail bookshop for the first time. How would you approach them?' If the recruit, with a gleam in his eye, said that he would acquaint himself with OUP's current and backlist, carry brochures of all the new books with him, along with a catalogue and an order book, Neil would mark his answer as wrong. He would then explain that a sales person had to first acquaint himself with the type of books and subjects that the shop he was visiting carried. This was then to be co-related to the OUP books in stock. On the next retail visit, only those books with their brochures should be carried to the shop for promotion. In this way, the sales person could make his calls more effective.

I was to remember this when Manzar came down to the branch office with brochures of a new book from Oxford, *The Oxford Companion to Wine*. He said the book retailed at 30 Pounds in the UK and Oxford was keen that all the offices make an effort to sell copies. I told Manzar to leave the cover and some sample pages with me. We were yet to receive an advance copy. I went the next day to the retail bookshop Teksons. The proprietor, Subhash Arora, was busy with customers, so I kept the cover and sample pages in a corner of the counter and made a beeline for the section which stocked books on wine. I immediately saw that Subhash had most of the books published by Michell Beazeley and quite a few by Hugh Johnson. Johnson was at the time the most prolific writer on wine. Our author was Jancis Robinson, one of the few women to hold a master's degree in wine. I knew Johnson had a contribution in Jancis's book. I also had a copy of his great praise for the book. The crowd thinned and Subhash came over, intrigued that I was spending so much time in the wine section. I told him we had a new companion to wine. Subhash's eyes lit up and he asked if he could see the book. I said we were awaiting the copy but I had the cover, sample pages and some advance reviews. I got them from the car and also showed Subhash Hugh Johnson's comments on the book. After I had told him the likely price we would retail it in India, he immediately placed an order for 300 copies if he was the exclusive distributor, or 150 if we were giving it to others too. Manzar was quite surprised at the response, but compulsions of all India marketing meant we could not go exclusive with Subhash. But Subhash established a market for the book and in the future too, he continued to order copies at regular intervals.

A year or so later, Jancis came on a visit to Delhi and called me through her cousin who worked at the British Council in Delhi. She thanked me for all I had done for the book and mentioned she had been invited to conduct a 'food and wine pairing' programme at the Oberoi Hotel and that the general manager of the hotel would call me. He did, and then asked me whom he should call, apart from his own staff. I suggested Dileep Padgaonkar, my friend and one of India's biggest journalists, who was a connoisseur. I told the Oberoi GM that I would also send some copies of the book for Jancis to sign. Dileep rang me up to say that he thoroughly enjoyed the programme. Jancis signed the twelve copies I had sent and they were all sold to the invitees at the event. Over the next few days, we had visitors to our showroom, the kind we had rarely seen before in those parts, wanting to buy books on wine!

*

In spite of Daryaganj becoming crowded, and parking virtually impossible on Ansari Road, book lovers continued to visit the OUP showroom. I had given instructions to the showroom-in-charge that I should be informed whenever academics visited, so that I could attend to them personally. Romila would usually come in with a set list of books which she needed to get. She would try to avoid seeing the new books I would recommend, but the temptation would prove too strong. Later, she would grumble good humouredly that she had a fixed budget and I always made her raise it. I would say, 'But what is a budget for a professor emeritus?'

I also derived immense pleasure from the visits of Professor Chandrasekhar Rao from Hyderabad. He often came to Delhi for meetings at the University Grants Commission (UGC) and would visit the showroom after the meetings were over. Sometimes, he would call me from UGC to say that he might be late and we would accommodate him by keeping the showroom open for an extra hour. He always spent his 'sitting fees' for the meetings on books. On one occasion, I had the satisfaction of showing him Samuel Finer's *The History of Democracy from the Earliest Times* (in three volumes) which OUP had published. It was a classic that he had been wanting to buy for a long time but hadn't found in any shop. He bought it immediately!

Upendra Baxi, the former vice chancellor of Delhi University and professor of law at the University of Warwick, was a frequent visitor and became a good friend. He used to buzz me from the phone in the showroom pretending to be a member of the staff. Of course I wasn't fooled, and we had a great time in the showroom selecting books. He always made a generous purchase and sometimes we could get into an animated discussion too—about books, universities, libraries and the future of education in India.

We had some memorable launches too at the showroom. It was our own place (though hired) and quite spacious. It was great to have a launch amidst so many books; our invitees too got an opportunity to browse after the function. The Jai Singh Road office would have been easier for people to reach, but space there was restricted. An even greater problem was that YMCA, which owned the building, was a little sticky about the serving of 'refreshments' in the evening as it was an institutional building. And how could we have a book launch for academics and booksellers without the stuff that cheers?

At one such launch, of the book *The Political Economy of Law* by Yash Ghai, Robin Lukham and Francis Snyder, we decided to have a slightly more elaborate function, with cocktails and snacks, as Yash had come down specially from Warwick for the event. My accounts officer, not favourably inclined to spirits of any kind, raised a few concerns about the cost exceeding the budgeted amount. I thought over the matter and then told him that I might have a solution. He was skeptical, for surely we were not expecting to sell enough copies of the book (it was a big one) to recover the costs of the party? I simply replied that we were going ahead and he should trust me. We had invited the eminent lawyer Soli Sorabjee for the launch, and after the programme I decided to take him around the showroom, making sure I steered him gently to the section where we had books on jazz. I knew Soli was a great jazz lover, and we had a splendid collection of jazz books published by our New York office. This list was entirely due to one particular editor in OUP New York for whom jazz was an abiding passion. Soli was quite surprised to see the books. He had a few in his collection but there were many more here. He asked me if they were for sale and on my affirmation, he made an extensive selection. He asked me if I could give him a good discount and whether the books could be sent on to his residence at Sunder Nagar the next day. I replied yes to both. New York gave us good terms on these books and I could part with a generous discount. The books were duly delivered to Soli the next day and his cheque for the amount more than compensated us for the launch party!

Let me end this memory piece on a wonderful books showroom with another 'post book launch' anecdote. We were the joint publishers, along with the Jawaharlal Nehru Memorial Fund (JNMF), of the *Selected Works of Jawaharlal Nehru* and Nehru's *Letters to Chief Ministers*. The latter collection was edited by G. Parthasarathy, the former diplomat and administrator who was better known as 'GP'. I had met him earlier when he had been the first vice chancellor of the Jawaharlal Nehru University (JNU), my alma mater. After the launch, I accompanied GP back to his car. On the way, I remarked on the democratic tenor of Nehru's letters to the chief ministers (he called them 'premiers') and how our present leaders could do well to emulate some of Nehru's grace and manners by reading his correspondence for themselves. GP smiled, but it was a sardonic smile, and it soon disappeared, as he snapped, 'Balan, let them get literate first.' This from someone who was considered a close adviser to two prime ministers, Indira and Rajiv!

WE SOLD *FANNY HILL* AT THE BOOK FAIR!

Publishers in India, particularly academic publishers, did not invest overmuch in either marketing or publicity till the mid 1980s. At OUP, for instance, the publicity function at the head office was looked after part-time by an editor who brought out single-sheet brochures on new books and did the annual complete catalogue which was more like a checklist of all the titles. In the branch offices a marketing person looked after the routine requirements of the sales teams and took out sporadic advertisements using zinc blocks. OUP did not publish modern fiction and did not have much by way of trade books, except dictionaries, the World's Classics series and a few imported titles from Oxford and New York, along with the Faber & Faber list. Since the major thrust of the publishing was on academic and scholarly lists along with a vast school list—the markets and readership for both were clearly defined—it was felt that there was really no need for marketing or publicity. We were all told, 'Just get the books out there and they will sell'.

This meant, of course, that books published or distributed by academic publishers were hardly visible outside the publishers' warehouses and showrooms, college libraries and the studies and dens of professors and research scholars. Very few retail bookshops stocked them. The general reader had almost no access to these books (this was long before online sellers appeared on the scene). Equally, there was no place where the editors and sales staff of publishers like OUP and Macmillan could see or interact with individuals who actually bought and read their books—the OUP showroom on Ansari road being almost the only little light in the dark. But there was also another, a much bigger light that shone every other year: the World Book Fair (WBF) in Delhi.

WBF was for years—and still is—one of the more important forums for publishers to interact with the book-reading public. Like many other publishers, both trade and academic, OUP had been an enthusiastic participant in the book fair right from its inception. From its modest beginnings in the Connaught Place central vista in 1972, the Fair had grown in size to become a bi-annual event at Delhi's famed exhibition space, Pragati Maidan (now demolished for 'modernization'). It became an annual event in 2012. The Fair drew participation from almost all publishers, big and small, including foreign participants. Organized by the National Book Trust (NBT) along with the then Trade Fair Authority, it occupied sizable space in Pragati Maidan and for ten days in February, the book fair became an integral part of the literary and cultural scene in the capital.

Ever since its inception, publishers have been enthusiastic supporters of WBF. This, in spite of problems.

The Fair was held usually in February—great weather in Delhi, but also the selling and promotion season for publishers, especially those involved in school education, and the Fair stretched their resources. Besides, there were always infrastructure problems at Pragati Maidan, the venue of the Fair, and Delhi being a 'bureaucratic' city seemed to care more for its high-ranking officials than for a book-loving public. All this notwithstanding, each year the number of participating publishers, in several languages, increased, with many coming in from outside Delhi.

A journalist friend of mine with more than an adequate knowledge of the trade once wrote a major article on the fair, titling it, 'We call it the World Book Fair, but does the world?' His point being, was WBF a calendar event among the international publishing community, and was it even close to the status of either Frankfurt or London?

The answer actually would be 'yes'. As WBF grew in stature and importance, international publishers began to attend. Sometimes, the publishers' delegations were so big that the British Council and the French Embassy began to host special receptions in their premises after checking that their dates did not clash. Today, the plethora of lit fests all over the country feature interviews with and write-ups on iconic authors. But during WBF, the features were on iconic publishers! The ten days of the fair were also full of publisher parties for their foreign visitors and the parties could run up to three or four a day! Delhi's pre-eminent stature was further confirmed with the International Publishers Association holding its first-ever congress in the capital in 1992, with some hallowed names from the publishing world attending (followed by another congress in 2018).

It was not very difficult to imagine why OUP and, more particularly the big trade imprints, would welcome participating in the World Book Fair. First, it afforded publishers a chance to exhibit their books at a wide square feet of space for ten days; hiring that kind of space in downtown Delhi would otherwise have been prohibitive. Secondly, WBF was a 'trade' fair, a commercial exchange place where publishers actually sold books to customers on an OTC (over the counter) basis. In this way WBF was—and remains—distinct from its counterparts in Frankfurt and London, where the major business was in transacting and selling rights. The members of the general public were allowed in only on the last two days of the Frankfurt and other book fairs. At WBF, thousands of individuals and families came to Pragati Maidan every single day of the Fair, to browse and buy. To encourage sales, NBT's condition to all participating publishers was that they must offer a standard discount of 10 per cent on all purchases.

Thirdly, and more importantly, the book fair was a means for publishers to be in direct contact with readers. This may seem surprising but it must be kept in mind that in India, most of the trade in books is done through distributors, both retail and wholesale, and it is they who are in touch with the customers. WBF enabled publishers to gain an insight into customer preferences and reading habits. Fourthly, this was a 'cash transaction' fair where the publishers actually collected cash against sale. This improved the cash flow position for publishers for the month, important in a trade where all the invoicing is done on a credit period and where collections could be problematic. Fifthly, WBF, like the equally famous Kolkata Book Fair, was a very good training ground for all sales staff, particularly the 'rookies'. It enabled them to get to know the publishing list better and they became trained 'hand-sellers'.

Each year, WBF saw increased footfalls and the enthusiastic crowds thronging the stalls gladdened publishers' hearts. But the month of February, as I've explained, was also a time for selection and serious buying by librarians and other staff of academic institutions, government agencies and public undertakings. They needed some peace and quiet in which they could make their selections. Soon, the organizers of the Fair had to reserve the forenoons of working days for 'trade and institutional' visitors only. The orders booked by these institutions and some upcountry visitors could be quite handsome indeed, as many had to exhaust their purchase budgets by the end of the financial year.

In the years that I have attended WBF (almost continuously from the year 1984), I tried to train the staff in actively 'promoting' books to customers rather than merely 'handing over' what they wanted to see. This experience of 'promotion', both to institutional visitors and to individual customers, would stand them in good stead in later years. Knowing exactly where particular books were located was very important as the staff would just get a couple of minutes to attend to a customer on a crowded day. In order to do this, it was compulsory for sales staff to be involved in stocking the bookshelves the previous day. The books were always arranged either by subject or category. The sales staff were helped by support staff but it was always chaotic as we barely had half a working day—and till late evening, if the Fair authorities allowed—to organize the books and get the stall ready before the inauguration. Not only sales staff, but colleagues from editorial, marketing, design, production and other departments would be at the stall until midnight. I have seen some publishing and sales directors on their knees, unpacking cartons and arranging books. There was a good deal of grumbling and criticism of the designer who was always putting things together at the last minute, but a dinner ordered and served to all working staff at the stall would put matters right. Yes, the stall was always 'designed' to provide for a better ambience to the customer. In addition to the design, many of the trade publishers would highlight their book of the year or their celebrity authors. Stalls also tried to provide extra seating and a coffee machine for the weary book lover. The Fair was taken seriously by publishers who used to look very critically at their location in the exhibition halls—how near or far from the entrance and exit, for instance. One felt happy if one was located near the major trade publishers for they were sure to attract maximum footfalls with 'standing room only' on weekends. A location near them would attract 'spillover' crowds into one's stall, much like the 'interceptor' stores in shopping malls.

OUP too attracted a good number of visitors to its stall. The selection of books to be exhibited was carefully done. Apart from major shelving devoted to the dictionaries which were always a popular draw, OUP made a major effort to display as wide a selection of its limited trade list as possible, especially from Oxford UK and USA and the Faber list. So, in addition to its academic list and the Oxford India Paperbacks, OUP displayed its World's Classics series, the illustrated encyclopedias, the Oxford anthologies in various subjects, the Oxford Companions, the Oxford Histories, etc. The Past Masters series too was given prominence, along with popular science titles by authors like Dawkins and Kaku. Space was also devoted to school books for selection by educationists. For some time that full magisterial 20-volume set of the Oxford English Dictionary (second edition) was displayed in all its glory as a 'collector's item'. There was a special price on it, for the customer was hardly going to see a third edition of the OED in print format! An institutional customer who picked this up always got a special applause along with a photograph. For individual customers, the Compact Edition of the OED was available with its own magnifying glass in a special case.

Care was also taken to display books by all the Delhi-based authors along with other authors who were likely to visit. Nothing pleased an author more than to see his or her book on display. Before the World Book Fair started the practice of interactive sessions with authors in 'author corners', publishers organized author visits to their stalls and special signing sessions. It was a thrill getting a signed copy from a favourite author. In the early years, it was possible to get authors like Ruskin Bond, Vikram Seth, Shobhaa De and even a V.S. Naipaul to the Fair and the crowds were still manageable. But for William Golding, we had to arrange a special signing session at a reception in a downtown hotel when he came visiting in 1986.

OUP in India did not publish modern fiction though it had dealt with that genre when it had acted as an agent for Hodder & Stoughton in the 1930s. It did carry a full range of the classics in its World's Classics range. Penguin was the acknowledged leader in the field with two sets of the classics, one popular and the other a black edition, which was more academic. But OUP's 'World's Classics' had a good critical apparatus, including a scholarly introduction by a noted authority. It was indeed a proud moment for OUP India when it published a World's Classics edition of the *Kamasutra* with a scholarly introduction by Sudhir Kakar and Wendy Doniger. Apart from this edition, the World's Classics published by OUP did not have any of the erotica that were also termed classics. These were the hallmark of Wordsworth Publishers, who were trying to make their presence felt in a market dominated by Penguin and OUP. To popularize their list in the market, Wordsworth would offer the seventh free on every purchase of six classics!

But once, a popular erotic work did—perhaps by accident—find its way onto OUP's World's Classics list. This was John Cleland's *Memoirs of a Woman of Pleasure*, or *Fanny Hill*. It was originally published in two instalments in 1748 and 1749. Even though the novel was written while the author languished in a debtor's prison in London, there is considerable speculation that at least a part of it was written when John Cleland was in Bombay working for the East India Company in 1740. At WBF one year, my colleague Thomas Abraham, who preferred our trade list to the academic, took charge of the World's Classics section. One afternoon, we found a whole group of Catholic sisters from an upcountry convent converging on our stall. After some time, Thomas came excitedly to us and said that one of the sisters had picked up a copy of *Fanny Hill* and after looking through it for a long time had placed it back. Thomas was convinced that she was interested in the book and he wanted to make a sale if possible.

We had an enterprising editor, Urmi Goswamy, in the stall on duty that day. She offered to station herself near the World's Classics section and Thomas discreetly moved away. Sure enough, the sister came back to the section now, a little encouraged and emboldened by the presence of a girl staff member. She again picked up the copy of *Fanny Hill*. Urmi now moved nearer. Finally, the sister turned to her and asked if the book was too 'bold'. Urmi answered that it was a classic and 'the prestigious Oxford University Press' had issued it as a 'World's Classics' edition after considering all aspects. Why, it even had a critical introduction by a scholar! This clinched the issue and the sale was made. For the record, though—and in defence of the venerable OUP—I must point out that *Fanny Hill* is a landmark work, being one of the first books of pornography written in the form of a novel. And there are no dirty words in the book at all; it uses euphemisms or lofty literary terms to describe body-parts and actions of the carnal kind. The 'highwrought agitation' of 'nethermouth' and 'furious fescue' cannot offend anyone. It is literature.

*

Let me conclude with another interesting WBF memory. This is from the year when Poland was the 'guest of honour' at the Fair and Ruskin Bond was invited to be the chief guest. In the presence of the Polish Ambassador to India, Adam Burakowski, Ruskin praised the contribution of Joseph Conrad to literature, mentioning that Conrad was Polish in origin. Later that day, I was able to talk to Ruskin as he spent the day with us (at the Ratna Sagar stall; I had moved on from OUP by this time). I told Ruskin there was another connection between Poland and India besides Conrad whose books were popular here. I said this went back to World War II. Ruskin was now intrigued, for he could sense a story. I told him what I had recently discovered: about one thousand Polish children had been displaced and left homeless and orphaned by the war. Many of their parents were victims of Nazi Germany, which had invaded Poland in 1939, and those that survived the war were shipped off to labour camps in Russia. About a thousand children and some families, however, managed to escape, and they travelled to India by a hazardous overland route, via Turkmenistan, Iran and Afghanistan. Some of them were taken in by families in Nagpur, Kolhapur and Bombay, but 640 children bereft of any family support, and some with special needs, found themselves without shelter. This was when the Jamsaheb of Nawanagar (now Jamnagar), Digvijaysinghji Ranjisinhji Jadeja, stepped in and offered refuge in his state. He provided them a home near his palace at Balachadi and also built a school for them. He even brought in cooks from Goa to prepare less spicy food for the children.

The children spent four years in India, from 1942 to 1946. When the war ended, they went back to Poland, but they never forgot their benefactor. The Polish authorities acknowledged the kindness of the Maharaja by naming a road and a school after him in Warsaw. Ruskin wanted to know more; he had a vague memory from his childhood in Jamnagar, of his father, who was a tutor to the Jamsaheb's children, telling him about young Polish refugees. I told him there was now a documentary on the whole story, *A Little Poland in India*, which I had recently seen at the India Habitat Centre. In 2017, when Ruskin published his autobiography, *Lone Fox Dancing*, he made a mention of this remarkable episode in Indian history.

I was to learn later that the road in Warsaw dedicated to the Jamsaheb was actually a crossroad, and it was called Skwer Dobrego Maharadzy (The Good Maharaja Square). And the Polish Ambassador whom I had met at WBF was a product of the Digvijaysinghji Ranjisinhji School in Warsaw!

BEHIND THE SCENES

Today, when the process of printing and binding a book is largely automated and computer controlled, not many would believe that there was a time, not so long ago, when these processes were largely done by hand. True, machinery drove printing even then, but behind the machinery, and even before the typeset matter was taken up for printing, master printers or craftsmen known for their knowledge and skills were at work. One such printer was P.K. Ghosh of Eastend Printers, Kolkata. Christopher Hurst, the legendary publisher and director of C. Hurst and Co of King Street, London, has written a wonderful book on the history and craft of book making, *The Invisble Art—The Pursuit of Book Making*. Hurst had a long collaborative association with Indian publishers, and for years, wrote a column, 'The View from King Street', in *The Hindu Literary Review*. The columns too got converted into a book and were also incorporated into his autobiography. *The Invisible Art* deals with the behind-the-scenes process of book making—how a manuscript is edited, marked up and made ready for the press, and what are the things to look out for and fix before it is taken on the machine. The book should be compulsory reading for all young aspirants in publishing and in courses on publishing.

In the Appendix to *The Invisible Art*, Hurst has a chapter on P.K. Ghosh, the 'Master-Printer'. Ghosh was born in 1917 in a village in Bengal and came to printing somewhat late in life. After a short stint in academics—he was a college lecturer for six months—he set up an advertising agency, which he ran from 1944 to 1951. In 1952, he finally found his true calling; he opened a small printing press, Eastend Printers. He invested in a limited range of type, Baskerville, Times Roman and Bembo, and got to work. He had to solicit for work in those days, and Hurst records that he approached the publisher Orient Longman, offering to typeset a manuscript on a 'trial' basis and not to charge them if they were disappointed with his work. It was the start of a long association with both this and other publishers. Though Hurst himself had the privilege of meeting Ghosh only in 1998, their association began in 1981, when the book *A History of Sri Lanka* was to be typeset in India and co-published by OUP. A lot was riding for Hurst on this book. Not only did he have English rights but had also tied up arrangements with a US publisher, and the Americans are nothing if not fastidious. Faced with restricted market rights, Ravi Dayal of OUP India insisted the manuscript had to be typeset in India to cut costs. Hurst chose Eastend Printers, having seen and approved some of their work for UK. OUP too finally went along with the decision, having worked with Ghosh before but did have initial misgivings about the limited range of type the printer had. The project was a brilliant success.

When I joined OUP later as an editor, I quickly realized what a formidable printer Ghosh actually was. For he was not just a typesetter and printer but an editor too. There was not much to editing, syntax and grammar that he did not know and his eagle eye was quick to spot what an editor had overlooked. To add to the hapless editor's discomfiture, Ghosh did not accept inadequate work readily, and what's more, would point this out in some detail. I quickly learned that your work had to 'qualify' to be typeset and printed by Ghosh. Ghosh passed away in the year 2000, and in a masterly tribute in *The Telegraph*, my former colleague and friend Rukun Advani mentioned his first book as an editor with OUP, *Elementary Aspects of Peasant Insurgency in Colonial India* by Ranajit Guha, which with some trepidation was sent to Eastend for typesetting and printing. Guha was then teaching in Australia and was to later become the editor of the Subaltern Studies series which became a landmark in scholarship. But his association with OUP began with *Peasant Insurgency*. As Rukun has written, 'Not only was Guha's language meticulous and highly polished, he was also known to be acerbic and touchy and even vitriolic.' It couldn't have been easy for a young editor to work on his book! Rukun's discomfiture was further heightened when P.K. Ghosh insisted that he would like to edit the manuscript again, and it was a very nervous Rukun who had to inform Guha. Guha replied by telegram that if 'Prabhatbabu' (Ghosh's full name was Prabhat Kumar Ghosh) was going to edit the script, he would be happy to wait. Rukun recalls that Ghosh soon spotted 'some solecisms and niggling problems of the sort that only strike Bengali intellectuals'! It was a stroke of luck that Guha too was one such intellectual, for he accepted all the changes suggested by Ghosh.

For those of us who were not brave enough to risk the wrath of the equally acerbic Ghosh, there was a great shield to hide behind: Dipen Mitra, the production manager at OUP. Dipen (who is still with us) was of the old school and his own knowledge of typefaces and composition equalled that of Ghosh. Many of us were fortunate that it was Dipen who decided whether our work qualified to be sent on to Ghosh. If a cursory glance assured Dipen it did, he then carefully edited it again and marked it up for Eastend Press. What followed was a communication, always in the form of letters, in which only the gods could intervene. We, the lesser mortals, merely stood on the sidelines, silent witnesses. Among the scripts that I remember being discussed in such fashion by Ghosh and Dipen was another one that Rukun handled, *The Unquiet Woods* by Ram Guha. This Guha was a little more easy of temperament than the other, but nevertheless, Rukun had a lot riding on this book too. We had sold US rights to Lynne Withey of the University of California Press, Berkeley, and she would buy our typesetting if it was done by Ghosh. The correspndence on this and on other scripts between Ghosh and Mitra was legendary. It was a classic exchange in the best of the Bengali 'Bhadralok' tradtion. Respecting the other man's expertise, Ghosh would suggest some changes, usually with 'Do you think this looks better?' or 'Do you think, this can be rephrased thus?—to be met with equally polite replies from Mitra either agreeing or rephrasing the text again. And so it went on, and what emerged were some very fine books. Rukun states that it was a humbling experience learning from Ghosh. It was equally so for us to learn from Dipen.

Dipen shared a passion for football, 'the beautiful game', with Santosh Mookerjee, another colleague, who succeeded Ravi Dayal as head of OUP India. During the 1986 World Cup, Dipen was one of the few I knew who would avidly watch the matches telecast at 12 midnight and at 2.30 a.m. and come in to office on time the next day. For quite some years, he lived nearby, and when we used to go to our respective cars after an OUP reception, he remarked that opening the car door was an 'acid test of our sobriety'. We had no remote electronic keys in those days, and the test was the insertion of the key into the door lock with a steady hand!

John Mackrell was a close associate of Dipen Mitra's at OUP, and we learned a lot from him, too, in terms of design, layout and production. A cartographer by training, he set up the cartography department in OUP India. After working briefly with OUP at Oxford, he had come out to India having seen OUP during a period of austerity after the war years. John married here, raised his family and almost never went back. He did go eventually, as his son would have better opportunities in the UK and his wife had retired from All India Radio. John finally retired from OUP, Oxford and then was hired by the Bodleian Library on a contract basis where he continues to this day, the contract being renewed annually. We were fortunate to have John travel to the press with us and iron out last-minute production problems. At an editorial-cum-production conference in Mumbai, John spent over an hour talking about the design of the preliminary pages (the prelims) in a book. His session should have been recorded for all trainee editors in the future.

In September 1988, OUP published the second and revised edition of the *Compact Handbook of the Birds of India and Pakistan: Together with Those of Bangladesh, Nepal, Bhutan and Sri Lanka*. It was a big book for us, almost 900 pages, with an extensive colour plate section. It was also a poignant moment for us, for Salim Ali had passed away the previous year and S. Dillon Ripley, the co-author and Secretary Emeritus of the Smithsonian, had come down specially for the launch. The launch was attended by the scientific adviser to the US Ambassador who, impressed with Dillon's presentation, placed an order for 50 copies of the book. After the launch, Dillon indicated to me that he had been invited for dinner at the adviser's home the same evening and it would be nice if the copies could arrive before he did.

Stocks of the book had just been delivered to our warehouse in Daryaganj and John and I undertook to 'check' the copies before final delivery. I had naively assumed we would need to just check 60-70 copies to get 50 good ones. I said as much to John, who merely smiled. In the event, we wound up checking over 200 copies to get 50 of good quality. I could not understand the high rate of rejection and said so. John then pulled out a copy of the book and asked me to look at the colour plates closely. I did and thought there was nothing wrong with them. John urged me to look even more closely and pointed out some lines across a few of the colour pages. 'These are brush marks,' said John. 'It's true that in some pages, they are not very discernible and are okay for the general market. But these will not do for the scientific adviser who is likely to donate them to scientific institutions.' Thus, we spent the better part of that afternoon going through the copies till John pronounced himself satisfied. I asked John the reason for the marks. He said in the binding unit the coloured sheets would have been laid out for drying after printing. In order to smoothen the pages, the staff, more often than not, used a broomstick to brush the pages. Unfortunately, as the pages were still wet, the stick left faint marks on some of the pages. The trick was to spot the pages without the marks. Another lesson learned 'behind the scenes'!

There are at least a hundred such lessons I can recount. But here's one that still boggles the mind. The Oxford Advanced Learner's Dictionary (OALD) was the bestselling ELT Dictionary in India and OUP reprinted it here under special licence from Oxford UK, subject to the condition that it was to be sold only in India and its adjacent territories and was not meant for export. It was also priced suitably for the Indian market. In the year 1989, a representative of UBS Publishers Distributors, while travelling to Russia, happened to secure a large order for the Indian edition of the OALD from the Russian authorities. Naturally excited, but knowing fully well that the edition of the OALD was not meant for export, he informed his boss Sukumar Das, the export director of UBS in Delhi. Learning that the order was for 50,000 copies, Sukumar called Santosh Mookerjee, then general manager of OUP India, and sought an appointment. A meeting between two venerable Bengalis who happened to be friends and shared a common passion for football could not be complete without the customary tea and 'biskoot'. But when Santosh learned the order was for the OALD, his face fell. However, after more cups of tea and 'biskoot', and as the order was large, Santosh was persuaded by Sukumar, and against his better judgement Santosh agreed to send a telex message to OUP Oxford for special permission to reprint. After some persuasion, Oxford agreed to a one-time permission to reprint for export and subject to their getting a royalty on the sale.

As it was a time-bound order, and UBS had already collected an advance against the order, it was necessary to print and bind all copies and ship them to Odessa, the destination port, as soon as possible. The printing presses in Delhi at the time being full, or at least the ones OUP used were full, a decision was taken to print and bind all copies in Calcutta and then send them by wagon to Bombay, from where they would be sent by container on a cargo ship bound for Odessa. This was duly done and knowing that the ship would take fifteen days to reach its destination, Sukumar sat back and waited for news of safe delivery of the consignment.

After the two weeks, Sukumar, to his consternation, received a telegram from the Odessa port authorities which read as follows: SHIP DOCKED stop. CONTAINER OPENED AND UNLOADED stop. TWO WORKERS FAINTED stop. COME AT ONCE stop. Sukumar immediately rushed to meet Santosh. This time, the customary tea and 'biskoot' were missing. The problem was of great concern because a majority of the workers at the Odessa port were women and the fact that two Russian women had fainted was serious indeed. A decision was quickly taken to fly the smartest sales executive in UBS at the time to Odessa. Though briefed beforehand, the executive was still not prepared for the scene at Odessa port, with the open container, books strewn around, and soldiers with guns at the ready. He quickly sized up the situation and gave instructions for all the books to be taken out and dried in the open. He took out a few himself to show that there was no danger. Finally some male workers did as he instructed, and after a couple of days, the books were ready for use. It turned out that as the printing and binding had been expedited and, thereafter, the books had been packed securely in an air-tight container, they had not had a chance to dry properly. The ingredients used in the binding glue at the time would give off a strong odour if not dried. Therefore, the container when opened, gave out an overpowering smell, worthy of anyone who would like to get 'high' by sniffing glue. In any case, it was concluded that the olfactory nerves of the poor Russian women were rather delicate and not used to strong odours, unlike the said nerves of their counterparts in India. It must be noted, however, that while this transaction was safely concluded, UBS did not receive a repeat order from the Russians.

Today, technology has successfully intervened in the binding process, and we have automated binding machines with mechanized trimming and stitching, and even the 'folding and gathering' of sheets is automated. The binding glue too has vastly improved in quality. Even the most delicate olfactory apparatus will withstand the scent of a book and the new 'hot melt glue' allows the book to be used minutes after application.

A GENTLE GIANT AMONG PUBLISHERS

DHANESH JAIN (1939 -2019)

In a lead feature published in the *Outlook* magazine, Dhanesh Jain, the Managing Director of the publishing house Ratna Sagar, described the Jains as a community that would give funds for the mere asking once the antecedents of the recipient were established. While the debate on whether the Jains should have accepted the 'minority' status granted by the then UPA government continues to divide the community, Dhanesh Jain himself would have explained the minority status as an enabler—it would help the Jains to give more to those in their community who are less fortunate, and to others too. During his lifetime, Dhanesh lived up to this axiom. But he gave quietly, without fanfare and fuss, benefiting numerous people, including the charities they were involved in. And he gave Indian school publishing perhaps its most astonishing success story—an entirely indigenous company that has set standards even the huge multinational publishers are trying hard to reach.

But he had to earn first in order to give. Dhanesh was born in Jammu, where his mother's family lived, but moved to Delhi along with the rest of the family and was educated at Hindu College, University of Delhi, and also did a project at the Fergusson College, Pune. The study of languages fascinated him and soon he enrolled himself for a PhD in Linguistics at the University of Pennsylvania. Duly completing his PhD with distinction, Dhanesh taught Hindi at UPenn for a number of years before moving back to Delhi. Continuing his interest in academics, he enrolled with CSIR as a Fellow and was seconded to teach at the newly opened Centre for Linguistics at the Jawaharlal Nehru University. The linguistics centre was not a 'high profile' department in JNU at the time. While Dhanesh loved the subject and interacting with students, JNU was a somewhat disorienting place, a hyperactive campus with students almost always in agitation over a host of issues, both domestic and international. Moreover, Dhanesh found the commute from north Delhi, where he lived, to south Delhi, where JNU is located, rather long and cumbersome on a two-wheeler.

The family had already initiated business enterprises. After discussions and knowing that his brother Rajinder would continue whatever was started, should he choose to do something else, Dhanesh resolved to set up a factory to make garment accessories, more specifically, buttons. But these were not ordinary buttons, they were to be high-end metallic and fancy buttons. Both brothers were convinced that there was a market out there for designer buttons. But first, Dhanesh had to learn the factory set-up and the manufacturing business. His wife Kusum Jain told me how determined Dhanesh was to learn, spending long hours driving up to Faridabad every day just to observe the systems and processes in a chemical factory. Soon, the buttons factory called Aero Enterprises was up and running and demand for the buttons started picking up. In order to speed up production, Dhanesh decided to import computerized machines from Milan, the only source for these machines then. The order books started filling up fast and, in some cases, demand would outstrip supply.

But Dhanesh was restless. His first love was still academics. He had teamed up with a distinguished scholar, George Cardona, to bring out a book on the Indo-Aryan languages and a publishing contract had already been signed with Routledge in the UK. Motilal Banrasidass, the publishers of Indology, were asking him to edit their series of publications on linguistics. He had also joined the Bhogilal Leharchand Institute of Indology in Delhi. He was to play a major role in the affairs of this institute later.

But the dilemma remained: how to combine business and academics? He was confident that his brother Rajinder and Rajinder's two sons would run Aero Enterprises very efficiently and take it to even greater heights, which they did. The output of the production line would be ordered almost a year in advance and on the days they sold on a retail basis, the retail counter at Sadar Bazar would see long queues.

For Dhanesh, getting into the publishing business offered a logical solution. It combined both books and business, in a way, his twin passions. His own son Sugat was studying then at IIT Delhi and after completion, was in line for an MS and a PhD in the USA. If the publishing venture did take off, Dhanesh hoped that in time, Sugat would return to help him run it.

So, in the 1980s, Dhanesh started his own market survey on the publishing industry and held extensive discussions with publishers who had impressive track records. He was also conscious that initially the funding for the new venture would come from the surplus generated from Aero Enterprises. In those days, commercial banks would not lend money to publishing enterprises (they still don't), considering the whole business too risky, and there were no bank overdraft facilities either. So, the initial seed capital was borrowed from Aero on a loan basis with an interest accrual.

Dhanesh soon realized that if he was to be up and running with a short gestation, it would be best if he could get into the textbook business. He chose to publish textbooks for the school educational programme in preference to that of the college, as the former had a more extensive market with two all India affiliating boards. We had no such standard syllabus for college education in the country with textbooks adopted in one region finding no takers in another. He also resolved early that if he was to make a decisive intervention in a crowded market with some of the biggest players in the business, his emphasis would be on a high level of content supplemented by 'state of the art' qualities of production. It was only through these that he could hope to have school principals to initially look at the books and later adopt them.

He therefore decided to approach publishing with a

missionary zeal, much like the missionaries of the cloth. His goal was to 'convert' the educational community to his way of thinking on education and eventually to his books. So, early on, he set 'Education, Our Mission' as the motto for the company. For the name and because of his academic interest he delved into history and came up with the three famous libraries of the ancient Nalanda University that had for centuries provided academic nourishment to scholars and travellers from so many countries. Among them, 'Ratna Sagara' was the most famous and accordingly Ratna Sagar P. Ltd was formally established and incorporated in 1982. The initial years were modest beginnings, with Ratna Sagar's first books meant only for the nursery classes. But Dhanesh had visualized a rather ambitious logo for the new venture. It depicted a shell (shankh) with sound waves emanating from it. It was drawn up by an artist and formally adopted to be used in all print books henceforth and in all stationery. In time, Dhanesh hoped the sound emanating from the Ratna Sagar books would send waves all over the country.

If we are to sum up Dhanesh's contribution to Ratna Sagar, three distinct areas emerge. One, he increased the visibility of Ratna Sagar on a pan-India basis. Ratna Sagar as a publisher of quality books began to be known in more schools as the sales team grew in confidence. For internal purposes, schools would be grouped on 'A', 'B' or 'C' basis depending on their location and on the resources they had. Dhanesh initiated a large number of training programmes for the sales team. He was careful to add training in 'soft skills' in addition to product knowledge.

This paid off quite well and as a result, after the initial emphasis—by necessity—on 'B' and 'C' schools, the teams began visiting a large number of 'A' category schools too.

Two, under Dhanesh, Ratna Sagar underwent a complete image makeover after some years. The training that he initiated internally, and this included support staff as well, was now extended externally. He realized schoolteachers often needed training to perform better. While most training programmes confined their ambit and scope to subject-training, Dhanesh extended it to motivation, parenting, counselling and even used teachers as catalysts to inculcate the reading habit among children. This resulted in Ratna Sagar being perceived among schools as a one-stop destination for all teacher training programmes.

Three, Dhanesh made Ratna Sagar a very congenial and agreeable place to work in. In its early years, Ratna Sagar had to face two problems. One was recruiting good staff to support expansion and growth. The other was retaining staff who had already been trained and had good product knowledge.

I shall take up the latter problem first. Existing staff were being lured by competitors who were offering better compensation packages. While Ratna Sagar did revise its own compensation, Dhanesh soon realized that the bigger players with greater resources could always offer more. At a meeting I suggested that perhaps we could turn the working culture at Ratna Sagar into an asset. Dhanesh himself was an embodiment of this. Democratic to the core and gentle in his dealings with staff, everyone was a valued colleague to him. He set very light store by hierarchy or designation. He preferred round-table meetings rather than with a head-table. Early on, he established an 'open door' policy to enable colleagues to meet him. He was clear that no one should be inhibited from making a point and that it would be heard. All line managers were given a great deal of autonomy and freedom to operate. For many years, sales staff did not have targets or budgets to achieve. At the risk of a little unpopularity, I had to initiate this by saying sales needed to work to targets.

Even if Dhanesh had to travel with teams together for meetings, travel was always together and in the same class whether by air or train and the same held true for the hotel accommodation. I distinctly remember travelling to a business meeting in Jaipur by the Shatabdi Express. The office staff through oversight had booked him and a few of us in the executive class and the others in the normal chair car. A visibly agitated Dhanesh got the tickets cancelled and all of us travelled by chair car. I sat with a motivated Kerala team and worked out the sales budget for the state on the reverse of the napkins served with our breakfast. When I showed this to Dhanesh, he remarked, 'You couldn't have done this sitting in the executive car!'

Accordingly, we began to have 'exit' interviews with those who wished to leave and those we wished to retain. Our emphasis on the working culture of Ratna Sagar paid off and quite a few stayed back and we redressed specific grievances. Our efforts at recruiting trained staff from other older and more established players got a boost when volatility and instability began rocking some publishing organizations. Ratna Sagar, in contrast, offered stability and continuity and many flocked to it.

Dhanesh's son Sugat joining Ratna Sagar after almost seven years at the University of Texas at Austin, thrust the organization towards innovation and modernization. It was he who introduced 2D and 3D animation into the books and has recently signed an agreement with Disney. An animation app was introduced which could be downloaded on to the mobile phone. The phone could then be used to scan a page in the text which had a sensor. When the page was played back on the phone, the visuals were animated. The whole page came alive and it greatly stimulated the child's interest. More recently,

Sugat introduced reporting from the school via an app. It was safe, accurate and quick and gave the line managers a quick fix on the executive's location. But as true as Dhanesh was, he first asked Sugat to explain the features of the reporting app to the sales team and get them to take up its ownership. For Dhanesh, ownership meant compliance and he said much the same about the sales budgets too.

Apart from the books and other educational materials, Ratna Sagar published something that was unique in the annals of Indian publishing. These were the annual 'Notebooks', first published in 1997 and continued ever since. These Notebooks were very dear to Dhanesh's heart and were a labour of love. They were not priced and hence were not for sale and Dhanesh insisted that they be distributed freely not only among educationists but also among well-wishers and friends. Each notebook centred around a theme handpicked for its uniqueness. Each chapter on some aspect of the theme was to be just a page in length with an illustration on its facing page. The chapter was not simply a body of facts but an interesting discourse enlivened with anecdotes. The themes included 'The Story of English', 'Indian Literature', 'The Journey of Indian Painting', 'A Journey to India ' and 'Shakespeare—400 years', to name a few.

The Notebooks soon became collectors' items, but sometimes they went further. A director of a leading school in Vishakapatnam told me she liked 'A Journey to India' so much that she had organized the school's annual day around the theme of the Notebook. The Notebook described the reactions of various travellers to India in history ranging from Megasthenes to Eric Newby. The children were asked to appear as each character from history and read an excerpt on India from the Notebook. They were thrilled to appear as Megasthenes, Ibn Batuta, Marco Polo and so on. Dhanesh was thrilled too, and kept publicizing this at our meetings. Similarly, the Notebook on Shakespeare published in 2016 to commemorate his death in 1616, led to a number of workshops for teachers on publishing history—'The amazing story of the First Folio', 'The influences on Shakespeare's writing' and 'Language, words and puns in Shakespeare'. The Notebook fascinated school principals in Hyderabad so much that they rehearsed and enacted the courtroom scene from *The Merchant of Venice*. This also led to an interesting debate on whether Shylock was more 'sinned against' than 'sinning', with one principal coming up to me to say that Shylock had been wronged by history. Dhanesh loved this and was rather pleased that school principals were thronging a workshop on Shakespeare organized by Ratna Sagar. This, above all else, provided ample testimony that Ratna Sagar had indeed arrived in the ELT world.

*

Dhanesh may have been a gentle spirit but he had a sharp and analytical mind; he missed nothing. His presence at our meetings gave them very clear intent and focus. Above all, facts were sacred to him and in analysis and interpretation, he did not like to see the facts themselves being changed. If an effort was made to 'embroider' poor results with elaborate reasoning and, in any way, 'mask' the facts, Dhanesh quickly saw through this and his remarks were often sharp and incisive. He would give his colleagues every opportunity to explain and improve later but the facts needed to be acknowledged and owned up to.

In this context, I would like to highlight an issue that is quite unique in the history of Indian publishing and one that deserves to be more widely known. Dhanesh, of course, appraised me of the case as soon as I joined Ratna Sagar in 2005, but the background and fuller circumstances of the case I have come to know only recently.

School textbook publishers rarely submit their books for review in the media. Space for book reviews is limited in the print media and most of it is taken up for reviews of books for general reading, both fiction and non-fiction. Moreover, the content of school textbooks was meant to cover the syllabus of a particular class and would not as such interest the general readership of a newspaper. But sometimes the content of some school textbooks became the subject of a news story, especially if something in the book was incorrect or controversial. The incident I'm recounting related to Ratna Sagar and the Times of India (TOI), then, as now, a leading and very widely read national newspaper. TOI did not have a dedicated book review page for weekend reading, unlike some other papers. Books got highlighted in the TOI more by default as it were. A few books were featured in Section Two of the city edition due to the interest of the editor at the time, and in the general paper, books got featured either in Mr Sham Lal's op-ed column ('Life and Letters') or in Dileep Padgaonkar's ('The National Scene'). This deliberate banishing of books, especially locally published ones, from its pages has been an old, and in my opinion valid, criticism of TOI. There are of course many others. But there was one remarkable initiative the newspaper took that deserves appreciation. In 1994, Justice P.N. Bhagwati, the former chief justice of India, was appointed as the *Times of India* ombudsman. This was the first initiative of its kind in any Indian newspaper. Grievances and complaints against the paper could now be referred to the ombudsman, and by appointing someone of the stature and integrity of Justice Bhagwati, TOI was indicating it had high professional and ethical standards, and was therefore beyond reproach.

On 9 January 1994, a report appeared on the front page of TOI, stating that a Class 3 social studies book depicted the people of a particular state, in this case Goa, in an unfavourable light. The report by a correspondent who possibly belonged to the same state, said the book showed the people of Goa as 'fun-loving' and fond of music and dance and also as 'westernized' (whatever that may mean). The report was titled 'NCERT book raises hackles in Goa', but the story itself was about a 'private publisher', not the National Council of Educational Research and Training, which is a government organization. And the report wasn't clear about exactly whose 'hackles' had been raised. It was quite misleading and mischievous.

Such a report can be extremely damaging to a publisher's reputation and image and can not only lead to loss of business but also to blacklisting by schools. The 'private publisher' referred to in the story was none other than Ratna Sagar.

While two executives were sent to Goa to do damage control, it was Mrs Kusum Jain who, after consulting Dhanesh, decided that redress had to be sought from TOI itself. Armed with the Social Studies books and with the TOI report, she went to see the then TOI editor in his office. He was out but she was fortunate enough to meet his personal assistant, who directed her to Justice Bhagwati's assistant. The latter heard her patiently and suggested that Dhanesh write a formal letter of complaint to the ombudsman with the relevant enclosures and promised that he would put it up to Justice Bhagwati when he returned to Delhi.

Dhanesh's carefully worded letter stated that 'the reporter did not have his facts correct, nor did he check them against the book referred to'. The reporter had implied that the book depicted the Goan ethos as 'westernized' and quoted from the text: 'All men wear trousers and shirts. The women wear dresses or skirts and blouses'. In his rejoinder, Dhanesh reproduced the complete section from the text: 'The men wear trousers and shirts. The women wear dresses or skirts and blouses. Along the Konkan coast, the men wear lungis and shirts. Women wear sarees.' Thus, Dhanesh pointed out, 'The men' was distorted to 'All men' and, worse, the passage was quoted selectively. The reporter had also attributed 'fun-loving' to the text, but the phrase did not appear in the text at all. The headline of the report implied that the book had NCERT's approval or endorsement, but, Dhanesh explained, nowhere in the book nor in any publicity material had Ratna Sagar claimed that the book was approved by NCERT; in fact, no such approval was even necessary.

Bhagwati's ruling as ombudsman, published in the TOI of 4 February 1994, shows what a mind with fine legal acumen can do. His report, 'Danger of being too close to Sources', was scathing. The first para dealt with the role of a newspaper and then with the principles of objective reporting: 'Newspapers earn and maintain their credibility among readers by ensuring that their journalists adhere strictly to certain well understood professional and ethical rules and standards'. Bhagwati then went on to elaborate and reiterate these at length. But his conclusion was telling: 'I regret to find that all these maxims have been violated in the publication of a report "NCERT book raises hackles in Goa" published on 9 January, the subject of a complaint before me... One can only infer that the reporter has chosen to fight someone's private battle (possibly a rival publisher's) and has used the columns of the *Times of India* for this purpose. I am sorry to say that editorial content has been lax. When a letter of complaint came from the publisher of the textbook, Mr Dhanesh Jain, the editors did well to publish it in a shortened form, but allowed the reporter to add a comment longer than the letter itself, justifying his story and raising new and irrelevant issues.'

It was Bhagwati's concluding remark that was most disturbing and perhaps also relevant for our present times: 'What has disturbed me most about the report is that it has not only made baseless allegations regarding matter in a school textbook but has done it in a manner so as to inflame feelings and create disaffection among communities over non-existent issues. I am asking the Editor to admonish the reporter who filed the story and to institute adequate controls to ensure that such reports do not get into the news columns in the future.'

Needless to say, Dhanesh was greatly heartened and encouraged by this ruling and wrote a personal letter to Justice Bhagwati to thank him.

*

Dhanesh Jain passed away, in the early hours of 31 March 2019, as he had lived; quietly, unobtrusively and without fuss. A senior publishing colleague remarked to me that in his passing, 'an era has ended'. Indeed. An era in publishing that started with small beginnings in a modest office in north Delhi's Mukherjee Nagar and has now grown into a veritable giant in Indian publishing, with an impressive turnover derived exclusively from an indigenous product range. Most publishing houses of this scale would have an imported product range to support their business, but not so Ratna Sagar.

Located in the heart of a commercial complex, the Ratna Sagar main office was not exactly in the most inviting or hospitable surroundings. Yet, the moment you stepped in, you were in a different world entirely. As a nervous candidate appearing for her very first recruitment interview later remarked to us, 'I could not imagine such an office here. I was greeted with a smile by gracious front-office staff, a glass of water appeared as soon as I sat down. I was offered tea or coffee and even lunch... And all this before I had been formally interviewed, and there was no way of knowing if I would be selected!' In addition to a hospitable front-office staff, Dhanesh believed in providing a congenial work environment where even the washrooms were kept spotlessly clean. During the years we ran a kitchen, the office lunch was simple, wholesome fare—without onion or garlic, it is true, but it tasted great. And if Dhanesh happened to have dropped in at the IIC earlier in the day, some goodies were sure to emerge either at the lunch table or at the ensuing meeting, followed by some delectable coffee, of which he was a connoisseur. Dhanesh had even made provision for instrumental music to be piped into the office rooms via speakers to create a better work atmosphere. And each year, two packets of 'gajak' made with special jaggery would be given to all staff to share with their families. The Diwali function was always special in the office. Each year, a bookseller from a different part of the country was honoured along with his or her family.

Dhanesh's legacy lives on in the traditions that he had set. His commitment to innovation continues too. While the school textbook publishing programme has been growing apace, in addition to bringing in digital content and animation to make textbooks more interesting for children, Dhanesh's son Sugat has been working on a new imprint, Offshoot Books, which has two streams, Offshoot Education and Offshoot Kids. While Offshoot

Education looks at subject learning in new and interesting ways, the books under Offshoot Kids contain stories with a 'twist in the tale'. Here we have classic tales like *The Emperor's New Clothes*, *Snow White and the Seven Dwarfs*, *The Princess and the Frog*, *Beauty and the Beast*, *Pinnochio* and *Rapunzel* in entirely new interpretations, with some zany endings. There are underlying messages, too, quietly and skillfully worked into each story.

There is also a 'twist in the tale' series for adults, done as graphic novels. Here, the aim is to retell the stories written by the great bard William Shakespeare himself. The idea, again, is to make Shakespeare fun and accessible for contemporary adult readers, who can then pass on their enthusiasm for Shakespeare's work to their children, students or younger siblings. In the series, some of Shakespeare's villains, for instance, gather at pubs with clever names like Shaken, Not Speared, and do what they are best at—drinking, grumbling, scheming and delivering long soliloquies. We are not sure if the Bard himself would approve, but the Offshoot team has a great deal of fun bringing these books out. All the work—the text, design, illustrations and formatting—is done in-house, under Sugat's supervision, and the books have found a ready acceptance in foreign markets, too.

And so, the Ratna Sagar story carries on. Yes, Dhanesh is no longer at the helm of affairs. But his motto, 'Education, Our Mission', continues in new and different ways. We thank our teachers on Teacher's Day every year; perhaps the educational community may pause and thank Dhanesh Jain too.

THE YOGI AND THE LAWYER

This essay deals with Vivekananda's years when he was still a yogi on a spiritual quest and had not yet become a swami. And how, almost a century after he died, a little story about him proved useful for a couple of men looking to sell some books. But let us start somewhere near the beginning, when the Swami was a student.

After schooling in Calcutta and Raipur, in 1879 Vivekananda, born Narendranath Dutta, secured first division marks in the entrance exam to the Presidency College, Scottish Church and Christian College in subjects like philosophy, religion, social science and literature. He finished his Fine Arts degree in 1881, and then completed his Bachelor of Arts degree in 1884. Vivekananda's early education had been composite and holistic. He had studied Indian and western art and literature, and received training in Hindustani classical music. Now in college he read the works of Immanuel Kant, Fichte, Spinoza, Hegel, Schopenhauer, Comte, Mill and Darwin. He was fascinated with the works of the English philosopher Herbert Spencer and even corresponded with him, and later translated Spencer's book *Education* into Bengali. Apart from his college education, Vivekananda also studied the Hindu scriptures, the Vedas, the Upanishads, the Ramayana, the Mahabharata and the Puranas. He was so erudite that one of his teachers, William Hastie, wrote, 'Narendra is really a genius. I have travelled far and wide but I have never come across a lad of his talents and possibilities even in German universities. He is bound to make his mark in life.' These remarks were to prove remarkably prescient.

But Vivekananda's early life, though full of promise, did not point decisively to the path he would take later. In his early youth, his interests were varied and eclectic. As a teenager, Narendranath had a prodigious memory and a capacity for speed reading and absorbing, and this applied to almost everything he read—scholarly texts, of course, but also novels. At a talk, he was able to quote verbatim pages from *The Pickwick Papers* by Charles Dickens. On another occasion, Vivekananda borrowed some papers by and books on Sir John Lubbock, astronomer, mathematician and banker and the first vice chancellor of the University of London. He returned all the material to the college librarian the very next day, saying he had read them all. Seeing the disbelief on the librarian's face, Vivekananda quoted extensively from the books and papers, and only then was the librarian satisfied that the young man was not lying!

In his early years, and before meeting Ramakrishna, in what was to be the turning point in his life, Vivekananda was influenced by the Brahmo Samaj, or rather its breakaway faction led by Keshub Chandra Sen and Debendranath Tagore. It was Tagore who told

Vivekananda that he had a 'yogi's eyes'. At this time, though, Vivekananda was experimenting with freemasonry and had become a skeptic, questioning Hindu beliefs on karma and reincarnation and also rejecting idol worship. Keshab Chandra Sen had carried his disenchantment with Hinduism even further by converting to Christianity. But when Sen met Ramakrishna Paramahansa, he was so captivated that he re-converted to Hinduism. It was an elated Sen who first urged Vivekananda to meet Ramakrishna. In an earlier instance, Vivekananda's college professor, William Hastie, while taking a class on Wordsworth's poem 'The Excursion' and trying to explain the word 'trance' that appears in it, had told his students that they should meet Ramakrishna at Dakshineshwar to really understand what being in a state of trance might be. Some of Hastie's students did go to Dakshineshwar, but it isn't clear if Vivekananda was among them. His first meeting with Ramakrishna, by most records, happened a little later, when the great mystic was giving a lecture at a friend's house. Ramakrishna asked Vivekananda to sing, and when the young man obliged, Ramakrishna was greatly impressed and advised him to take more formal instruction in music. Later, Vivekananda was to learn Dhrupad and also the basics of playing the pakhawaj.

In late 1881, Vivekananda visited Ramakrishna in Dakshineshwar in what was to be a 'turning point' in his life. A skeptic, at first he questioned Ramakrishna's worship of Kali and was dismissive of his ecstatic, trance-like states and his visions of God, calling them hallucinations. He even questioned Ramakrishna about how clearly he could see God, and Ramakrishna, with a twinkle in his eye, said, 'As clearly as I can see you!' He urged Vivekananda to open up his mind and see the truth from all angles. Vivekananda's visits to Dakshineshwar became more frequent and once when financial troubles beset his family, he asked Ramakrishna to pray to the goddess Kali for him. Ramakrishna asked Vivekananda to do so himself. Sitting before the image of Kali, in deep meditation, Vivekananda underwent a spiritual transformation. He now accepted Ramakrishna as his master and tried to learn all that he could as an ardent disciple. Ramakrishna, in turn, saw enormous potential in Vivekananda, who became his closest disciple. Knowing his own end was near as he had developed throat cancer, in 1885 Ramakrishna initiated Vivekananda and a few other disciples as monks. Ochre robes were now to be Vivekananda's clothing and Ramakrishna also made his young disciple undertake a padayatra throughout India in order to understand its people better. Ramakrishna died in August 1866 and on the shoulders of the young yogi, who had not yet become a 'swami', fell the responsibility of carrying forward his master's message and working towards a spiritual reawakening of India.

*

In late 1886, Vivekananda and his disciples took formal monastic vows and set up a monastery in Antpur village. While Vivekananda prepared himself spiritually along with his disciples to undertake the padayatra to the north and the south of India, to touch the soul of India as it were, he realized he was now a Parivrajaka, a wandering monk. He gave up almost everything he owned. His entire possessions now were a kamandalu (water pot) and two of his favourite books, *The Bhagavad Gita* and *The Imitation of Christ*. Eventually, these travels within India between the years 1888 and 1893 were to prepare him to attend the World Parliament of Religions conference in Chicago in September 1893, where he is said to have given a sensational, transformative address. Meanwhile, his engagement with learning, education and music continued.

In education, Vivekananda favoured an inter-disciplinary approach and wished students of science to have some grounding in philosophy, history and so on. Not many are aware that he inspired Jamshedji Tata to set up what was then known as the Tata Institute of Science and is now more famous as the Indian Institute of Science. The Vivekananda Archives contain a fascinating account of this.

In July 1893, Vivekananda happened to talk to Jamshedji Tata on board the SS *Empress of India* bound for Vancouver from Japan. Vivekananda was en-route to Chicago to attend that celebrated World Parliament of Religions. Although Vivekananda was sixteen years his junior, Jamshedji could not help but notice his passion and intensity. Vivekananda asked Jamshedji to strive towards self-reliance in manufacturing. Why, for instance, was Jamshedji importing matches from Japan? Could they not be made in India? Vivekananda also spoke about a holistic and integrated education, emphasizing that it was the only means by which the Indian people could rise above poverty and make meaningful lives. The two men parted company at Vancouver, but Jamshedji never forgot this conversation. He was to also testify later that the Japanese had been captivated by Vivekananda, comparing his likeness to that of the Buddha.

But it was at the World Parliament of Religions in Chicago that the assemblage and the world at large saw the power of Vivekananda's eloquence. Originally invited by John Henry Wright to give a talk at Harvard University, it had been suggested that Vivekananda should also attend the World Parliament of Religions. But in order to be invited, he had to send an application to the selection committee. Vivekananda duly did so, introducing himself as 'a monk of the order of "sanyasis", an order founded by Sankara'. The presence of a Brahmo Samaj representative on the selection committee clinched his invitation. Initially nervous, Vivekananda began his address in Chicago with 'Sisters and Brothers of America'. He went on to greet 'the youngest of the nations' on behalf of 'the most ancient' order of monks in the world—'the Vedic order of sannyasis of Hinduism, a religion which has taught the world both tolerance and universal acceptance'—and then gave a short but scintillating speech on India and Hinduism. He got a standing ovation from the 7000 odd delegates. The next day, the *New York Herald* noted that Vivekananda 'is undoubtedly the greatest figure in the Parliament and after listening to him, we feel how foolish it is to send missionaries to this learned nation'.

Vivekananda returned to India in 1897 and his new

friend Jamshedji, elated by his success, wrote to him to prepare a pamphlet exhorting the youth to take up the study of science as well. Jamshedji informed Vivekananda of his intention to set up a research institute of science. But Jamshedji's hopes were rudely shattered by Lord Curzon when Jamshedji and Burjor Padshah went to meet him in December 1898. Curzon, still nursing the legacy of Macaulay that the educational system in India should create a nation of subalterns to help the British in their rule, rejected the idea of an institute where philosophy, ethics, metaphysics and psychology would be taught along with the natural and biological sciences. Short of saying that Indian students were incapable of studying these subjects, Curzon expressed serious doubts about the number of students who would come and whether they would get jobs later, and finally posed the clincher that there would be a dearth of competent teachers. Curzon appointed Sir William Ramsay to go through Jamshedji Tata's proposal. Ramsay echoed his master's view and said that philosophy and education could not be taught in a science university.

With Vivekananda's encouragement, the Ramakrishna Mission fully supported the idea of a research institute. In 1900, Vivekananda set out on his second foreign tour, this time accompanied by the teacher and social activist Sister Nivedita, who had met Vivekananda in London in 1895, become his disciple and moved to Calcutta. Nivedita knew of Vivekananda's desire to see the institute through and decided to drum up support in England. Nivedita had been a popular teacher in Wimbledon and along with

Ole Sera Bull, an American feminist, she approached the educationist Sir George Birdwood for support. Hearing of Tata's proposal, Birdwood rejected it out-of-hand, saying it would not be possible for Indians to run such an institute. Birdwood gave the examples of the universities of Calcutta, Bombay and Madras which were all in poor shape. Calcutta University, the oldest among them, he said, had not produced a single outstanding scholar. Poor Birdwood was on weak ground here. Nivedita, formidable and feisty, countered by saying that the British ran these universities and were therefore wholly responsible for their state, good or bad. As for Calcutta University, she said, perhaps Sir George had overlooked the eminent scientist Jagdish Chandra Bose, who was a product of that university. Bose had just delivered a brilliant lecture at the Science Congress in Paris and was touring England at the time. 'Moreover,' Nivedita went on, 'even the Royal Society has allowed full library facilities to Bose!' Nivedita even told Birdwood that Bose would head the planned research institute, confident that Vivekananda could persuade Bose to do so.

Birdwood did not budge, and Nivedita now wrote to several other intellectuals and educationists to support the idea of the institute. Quite a few of them did. Notable supporters were William James, the psychologist, and Patrick Geddes, the famous town planner, biologist and educationist. They wrote letters to Nivedita expressing complete confidence that the new institute of science would acquire an individuality and reputation of its own. (Geddes was to later write a biography of Jagdish Chandra Bose.)

The pressure on the British government to clear the science research institute mounted. Jamshedji, whose hopes had now been rekindled, invited Vivekananda to travel to Bombay. But Vivekananda, in poor health, declined the invitation with regret. He had had a premonition that he would not live to see forty. In the event, Vivekananda died in 1902 in his thirty-ninth year, and Jamshedji himself passed away in 1907. But Jamshedji did have the satisfaction of seeing at least the beginning of the process that would lead to his dream being realized. In 1905, the British government finally cleared the proposal for the research institute, and in 1907, the Maharaja of Mysore, an ardent admirer of Vivekananda for long, gave the land to fulfil the cherished dream. The Indian Institute of Science was established in Bangalore in 1909 on 800 acres of land. Old timers even now refer to it as the Tata Institute.

*

The Maharaja of Mysore had met Vivekananda during his padayatra of southern India to get to know India and its people better. Vivekananda was in Mysore as a guest of the Diwan of Mysore, K. Seshadri Iyer, in late 1892. It was the Diwan who arranged for his audience with the Maharaja and the latter was very impressed with the young monk's erudition and eloquence. In Mysore, Vivekananda heard about the deep-rooted caste prejudices in Kerala and the practice of 'untouchability'. Appalled and outraged, he called Kerala a 'lunatic asylum', and felt the people there were quite mad to practice such discrimination against their fellow-men. He decided to see the extent of the inhuman practice in Kerala for himself. But there was a small problem. Kerala was not in his original itinerary and he had made no arrangements for such a journey. The Maharaja came to his rescue and provided rail tickets for Vivekananda and his followers to travel to Shoranur. He also gave Vivekananda a letter of introduction to the Diwan of Cochin.

There are enough accounts of Vivekananda's travels through Kerala. He travelled through Thrissur, Kodungallur, Tripinithura and Ernakulam, moving on to Tiruvananthapuram, Nagercoil and Kanyakumari. At Kanyakumari, no boatman was willing to row him across a turbulent sea to a rocky outcrop. Undeterred, Vivekananda jumped into the sea, swam across and meditated on the rock. His three-day meditation on the rock was to turn the rock into the famous Vivekananda Memorial that now draws visitors from all over the world.

During his journey through Kerala, Vivekananda saw the caste practices, argued with Hindu pundits about their rationalization for these practices and even met a disciple of the reformer Narayana Guru, who had played such a major role in trying to eradicate untouchability. But it was an experience in Ernakulam that showed what a multifaceted and versatile genius Vivekananda was.

On 7 December 1892, Vivekananda and his followers were passing through Ernakulam town when they heard melodious music in the classical Carnatic style. Entranced, Vivekananda asked his followers to stop and listen. The song being sung was the famous 'Ashtapadi' composed by the twelfth-century composer Jayadeva. It is said that when Jayadeva sang the composition, his wife Padmavati was captivated, as if in a spell, and danced to it.

Vivekananda too listened entranced, his body swaying rhythmically. After the song ended, he made inquiries and learned the house was that of a prominent lawyer, Doraiswamy Iyer, a gifted singer. Honoured by the Maharaja of Cochin, Doraiswamy Iyer was also known as 'Todi Doraiswamy Iyer' because of his mastery over the raag 'Todi'. Vivekananda entered the house and urged a surprised Doraiswamy to continue singing. He even joined the celebrated singer now, and sang songs in Bengali. As the hour was late, Doraiswamy requested the young monk and his companions and disciples to eat and rest for the night in his house. The next day, Vivekananda and his followers continued on their way.

I was to relate this story to another monk over a hundred years later, when I was taken to the Ramakrishna Mission Boy's Home and school at Rahara in Calcutta by a colleague from the sales team of the publishing house I was working with. The headmaster, a practicing monk, indicated he could spend very little time with us. As my colleague was keen on getting some business in the school, I thought, 'Nothing ventured, nothing gained', and plunged into the story of Vivekananda's evening of music with the lawyer in Ernakulam town. The headmaster-monk listened with great interest. At the end, the astonished monk asked me how I knew the story, and in such detail that it appeared new even to him!

I told the headmaster-monk that the lawyer Doraiswamy Iyer who had been honoured by the Maharaja of Cochin with the 'veera sringala', and later had a road in Ernakulam named after him, was none other than my wife's great-grandfather! While the Malayalam newspapers of the time had carried an account of Vivekananda's encounter with Doraiswamy, I was alerted to the story by my wife's uncle who had carefully preserved a cutting of *The Hindu* which stated that Vivekananda had spent the night in the house of a prominent lawyer, Doraiswamy Iyer. In addition, there was a family account which gave further details—some of these unavailable even in the Vivekananda Archives, which carry an account of Vivekananda's travels in India (now in published form) by Shyamali Chowdhury, who writes that Vivekananda met 'a prominent lawyer, Doraiswamy Iyer' who sang the 'Ashtapadi'. The Ramakrishna Archives too have an account of Swami Ramakrishnananda, a direct disciple of Ramakrishna, who visited Doraiswamy at his house sometime after Vivekananda passed away. At the house, the swami told Doraiswamy that his house had now become a tirthasthan (holy place), and after inquiring from Doraiswamy where Vivekananda had sat, eaten and slept, the swami went around and prostrated at each of the places.

At Rahara, the visibly moved headmaster-monk corroborated the story and informed me that in later years, a succession of monks from the missions at Belur Math and Dakhineshwar would travel to Kerala while retracing Vivekananda's padayatra and visit Doraiswamy's house in Ernakulam. It had indeed become a tirthasthan. 'What happened to the house?' he asked, wondering if the holy place was still in the possession of the family. I sadly told him that it had been acquired by the Department of Fisheries of the government of Kerala and was later demolished. He sighed, but shook my hand excitedly. We had now spent forty-five minutes together. We left with my colleague quite excited, as it augured well for the future—with Vivekananda's blessings, some of our books would find a home in the Rahara school!

THE GODS BESTOW A FAVOUR

It was a book that sparked off a historic meeting that laid the foundation of political and cultural ties between independent India and France. While imprisoned in Naini jail during the freedom struggle, Jawaharlal Nehru had read a review of *La Condition Humaine* (*The Human Condition*) in the *New Statesman*. He had read the novel soon after, and been greatly impressed. The author of the novel was Andre Malraux and Nehru resolved to meet him whenever the opportunity presented itself. While attending to an ailing Kamala in Switzerland in the mid 1930s, Nehru hoped he might get a little time to dash to Paris to meet Malraux.

But first, a meeting had to be set up, and who better to do this than Raja Rao, the celebrated writer? Raja Rao had started his literary career at the age of fifteen, initially in Kannada and later in English. Though Kannada was his mother tongue, he felt he could not express himself adequately in this. His knowledge of Sanskrit was not good enough and thus for Rao, 'English remained the one language, with its great tradition and its unexplored riches, capable of catalyzing my impulses and giving them a near-native sound and structure.' But Rao always acknowledged his early debt to Kannada. He had published his early stories in Kannada periodicals and this literary output enabled him to adopt a more vigorous and authentic style which stood him in good stead for writing in English as well. His early writings impressed Patrick Geddes, the polymath scientist, sociologist and urban and town planner, who later was to be involved in urban planning in India. Geddes invited Rao to the new international college he had started in Montpellier in southern France. Many years later, Rao was to recall that the letter from Geddes, which came to him in a blue-covered envelope, had changed his life. The move to Montpellier was the beginning of a journey that would eventually lead Rao to spend more years outside than in India. Though Rao was proud to be Indian, he felt that his 'karma' had destined him to spend half his life outside his country.

In those early years, Rao found France much like India, formal and informal, friendly and chaotic. He was impressed by the self-reflectiveness of the French language and its musicality. He resolved to start learning it. He soon moved to Paris to continue his studies at the Sorbonne and later served on the editorial board of the *Mercure de France*, a French periodical, for seven years. It was during this time that he first met Andre Malraux. Rao's published stories attracted the attention of writers like Romain Rolland and Stefan Zweig. In 1938, Raja Rao published his most famous novel, *Kanthapura*, set in a south Indian village and written in a thirteenth-century castle in the heart of the Alps. It was praised lavishly by

E.M. Forster and Malraux, among others, and established him as a writer with an international reputation.

But *Kanthapura* was still a couple of years away when Nehru sought Raja Rao's assistance in arranging the meeting with Malraux. But Rao did, of course, know of Malraux, already a legend in France and the rest of Europe. Though it was the engagement with the human condition that was the common link between Malraux and Rao, Malraux being more of an adventurer, engaged with it in a more direct, forthright manner. As Rao put it, 'Malraux's love of revolution was spiritual, a love of pure greatness.' At the age of twenty-one, he went to Cambodia to discover the Khmer temples. In 1925, he went to Saigon to join the Young Annam League fighting against French domination. He joined archaeological expeditions in Afghanistan and Iran and his explorations in the Arabian hinterland for the lost city of Sheba made him famous. Malraux also fought for the Republicans during the Spanish Civil War. He organized the air force for the international brigade and was wounded twice. He was also one of the few persons allowed to be present in the room when Picasso worked on his famous painting *Guernica*. During World War II Malraux led a French tank unit and twice managed to escape German captivity. Malraux was involved with the Chinese revolution as well, but Stalin's excesses in Russia finally led to a disenchantment with communism.

Rao engaged with the world around him and the human condition very differently. He shared with Malraux an abiding love for the French world view, which he considered to be at the heart of western civilization. But for him, the search to improve the human condition was both philosophical and spiritual. In 1933, the same year that Malraux published his *The Human Condition*, on one of his visits to India from France, Rao stayed at Pandit Taranath's ashram in the Tungabhadra region. In 1942, he lived for a brief period in Gandhi's ashram, Sevagram. In the same year, he met his spiritual guru Sri Atmananda in Trivandrum. Above all, Rao was deeply influenced by Ramana Maharshi and tried to spend some time with the sage whenever he visited India.

Now Raja Rao had been tasked with arranging a meeting of Malraux with Nehru. Malraux's *The Human Condition* had won the prestigious Goncourt Prize in 1933, and had been translated into a number of languages. The novel was based on the early days of the Chinese revolution, more specifically the Shanghai Uprising of 1927, and depicted characters, including foreigners, who lead the people to rise up against their colonial masters, but are then finally betrayed and the uprising is put down. The novel also dealt with the early years of Chiang Kai-shek, who started as a heroic revolutionary but finally betrayed the cause and was forced into exile. *The Human Condition* received widespread publicity with the Goncourt Prize and many people began to identify with the Chinese struggle and with the main protagonists depicted in the book. Malraux was the toast of Europe.

Raja Rao soon realized that arranging a meeting with Malraux was next to impossible. Malraux was then the tallest literary figure in Europe. In contrast, Nehru was almost a nobody outside South Asia. He was still far from becoming the symbol of a freedom movement that would inspire the liberation struggles of Afro-Asian nations and make him well known internationally. Besides, Raja Rao knew Malraux but not well enough to arrange the meeting. But as Rao said, '…for an Indian nothing ever seems impossible. The Gods always work for you.' Finally, the meeting was arranged by Jean Guehenno, who edited the international literary magazine *Europe*, to which Malraux had contributed. Guehenno had also published some of Rao's early writings.

The historic meeting took place at a Chinese restaurant, The Shanghai, in Paris in January 1936. Even at the restaurant, Malraux was besieged by patrons and serving staff for his autograph. At the meeting, it was Malraux who appeared more in command. Nehru appeared tentative and hesitant. Nehru understood some French and Malraux some English. Rao was to be the interpreter but Malraux spoke so rapidly and animatedly that it was almost impossible to translate. Rao felt that for Malraux ideas were supreme and unless one could die for an idea, it was not worth living.

Malraux's first question was on Gandhi's philosophy. 'I am, as you know, interested in Gandhism. I can understand any intelligent man's aversion to violence. But I am an occidental man. I believe in action and in Europe, we are all in a hurry. But you, Monsieur Nehru, you are of the east. In India you have the window on eternity. So my question is what relationship has metaphysics with non-violence?'

Urged by Nehru to elaborate, Malraux went on. 'You in India have grown a civilization. You, sir, have created the Upanishads and the Gita, where Sri Krishna says: Standing beyond duality, you, Arjuna, kill and be killed, for in the end there is neither the killer nor the killed.'

Nehru remonstrated very quietly and deliberately. 'But Krishna tries every politic way to stop the war non-violently.' He pointed out how Gandhi, the apostle of non-violence, had offered to raise volunteers for the British army during World War I. In answer to Malraux's question as to why India had fought the British, Nehru replied Gandhi-like: 'To convert the enemy.'

And so it went on. Malraux concluded, 'Please never forget us, Monsieur Nehru. Remember me. I promise to visit you when India is free and when you become the prime minister of India, for Mahatma Gandhi will never become an official of any government. He is too much the chief of all men. Remember me and let me tell you finally what I have to say. Let the great Sankaracharya, let him guide India. Such is my prayer.'

Malraux was to keep that appointment with India. In 1958, de Gaulle, the French President, sent Malraux as his emissary to meet Nehru, now the prime minister of free India and one of the world's great leaders. Malraux had asked Raja Rao to accompany him. Nehru now appeared confident and seemed to be in command. To a very large extent, Malraux's visit was to allay India's suspicions about France, much to do with India's perception that France was more closely aligned to China. De Gaulle wanted to reassure India that France was its friend and who better to do this then Malraux, his trusted lieutenant? Malraux was the minister for culture in France and told Rao that in cabinet meetings, de Gaulle would never allow ministers to mention India and China in the same breath. De Gaulle believed that France was closer to India both philosophically and culturally. This is indeed significant, for the Malraux-Rao visit in 1958 helped to lay the foundation for a Franco-Indian cultural partnership that endures to this day.

In his autobiography *Anti-Memoirs*, Malraux mentions that Nehru had referred to Victor Hugo's *Les Miserables* as one of the most popular books in India. Nehru was deeply interested in Malraux's designation and spoke about his own intention to set up a department of culture that would broaden cultural ties between India and the rest of the world. Nehru realized that India was a newly independent nation which did boast of an ancient civilization, but it was not a great power either economically or in terms of military prowess. If it was to take its rightful place among the comity of nations, it had to do so culturally.

The meetings between Nehru, Malraux and Rao in 1958, which began in Nehru's parliamentary office, continued in his official residence and finally concluded in the French embassy, were indeed historic. On the one hand, they helped Nehru gain insight not only into French culture but also into France's attempts to build up a modern nation emerging from the destruction and debris of World War II. On the other, these meetings also helped Nehru to formulate a cultural policy vis a vis the rest of the world. India's foreign policy was just getting formed and Nehru realized that forging cultural links would greatly help in India getting closer to, and appreciated among, the nations of the world.

Andre Malraux travelled across India during that historic visit. Rao records that on Malraux's return to Delhi, Nehru asked him what he had seen of India. Malraux answered softly, 'Ajanta, Madurai and Nehru.'

When Malraux was in Madurai, arrangements were made for him to visit the famous Meenakshi temple. There is a photograph—now iconic—of a garlanded Malraux receiving the traditional blessings on his forehead. Finally, the man of action from the west, the 'occidental man', always in a hurry, appeared to have come to terms with, and submit to, a time-honoured ritual of the east.

READING IN TIRUNELVELI

Tirunelveli town in Tamilnadu may not appear to be the kind of place where you would expect to make substantial book sales, although it does have a fair number of schools, enough for it to be of interest to textbook publishers. The town is known primarily as the locale for a few blockbuster Tamil movies, and for its temples and waterfalls. It is even more famous for its delicious halwa. The most popular shop selling the halwa is known as Irrutukadai, or 'the dark shop'. Krishna Singh, a migrant from Rajasthan who opened the shop sometime in 1930, used to prepare the halwa in the morning, and since it required six hours' cooling time, he could open the shop to customers only in the evening. The halwa was served in the dim light of candles or kerosene lamps, hence the adjective 'irrutu' or 'dark'. Even though his successors, Bijli Singh and Hari Singh, replaced the lamps with electric bulbs, and production is now mechanized and no longer done by hand, the shop maintains its tradition of catering to customers only in the evening. Demand still far outstrips supply. Long queues are formed well before the shop opens. To cater to the increased demand for halwa, many competing stores have opened in Tirunelveli, and they serve the confection in the morning too. It is available online as well. But residents of the town still swear by the quality of the original irrutukadai halwa, and because it is scarce, the saying goes, 'Don't trust anyone who promises you Tirunelveli halwa, he's bound to give you the slip.'

Lured by the prospect of the elusive halwa, on an official trip to Madurai some years ago, I agreed to take a detour and visit some leading schools in Tirunelveli and its district. In the end, I was glad I made the detour; it was a wonderful experience, the highlight being my visit to Kings School in Vallioor village, which had both matriculation and CBSE streams. I was quite impressed with the school's architecture and its landscape, with gardens and streams. I surmised that someone who cared about the environment and loved nature had designed it to inspire the children and fill their days with beauty even as they studied and prepared for the world.

I was taken around the school by a proud principal who gave me a short history of the school. I learned that the school was the brainchild of Colin Wagstaff, who had set up a charity in England, the Kings World Trust for Children, in 1994. Colin's family had been associated with India for over five generations and Henry Lawrence, one of his ancestors, had started the Lawrence School in Sanawar. Colin's motto for the trust was 'Freedom from Poverty through Education'. Moved by the plight of a poor boy who had come to England for medical treatment, Colin resolved to help other young people in the boy's village in Tirunelveli. He initially set up a children's village. The Kings School was established in 2005, as a result of persistent demand from the villagers for an English-medium school where their children could receive quality education. It was only through generous donations by a number of benefactors in England and elsewhere that Colin was able to buy the land, about 50 acres, and build the school in stages. Starting initially with just nineteen students, the school now has over two thousand.

A high point of the visit was the Chris Bake Library. It was unlike any other school library I had visited. Not only in terms of its architecture and design, but also in the way the shelves were designed, to create maximum space for children to move around and browse. For more detailed study, there were reading tables. Going to the shelves, I was amazed at the stock of books. The library had the complete set of the Oxford English Dictionary (OED), all 20 volumes of the second edition. It had a complete set of the classics, both Penguin and Oxford editions. It also had a range of books by international and Indian authors, both past and contemporary. Its reference section was comprehensive, too. Clearly, someone had taken great pains to equip the library and the holdings went far beyond the requirements of a school education.

The principal informed me that the library was Colin's brainchild. Chris Bake was a very generous donor to the trust and hence, Colin decided to name the library after him. Colin himself supervised the library purchases, and in addition to the school textbooks and reference books, he felt that the library should have material to serve the needs of the children in the future too, in a fast-changing world. This was in keeping with Colin's motto that he wanted the children to 'learn' and not merely study. 'It took nine years for us to do the right thing by our children, so that they have the momentum to do whatever they want later in life,' the principal told me, quoting Colin. 'What does a high school graduate need to know and be able to do in order to thrive in college, the work-place and life in the decades ahead?' This was the question that guided the evolution of the school and its remarkable library.

Interacting with the librarian and seeing some children brought in by their teachers, I learned that while library time was one period per class per week, the principal's wish was that the library facilities should be more frequently used. The school had boarding facilities for both boys and girls, and the principal was keen that I should take a programme on reading to not only interest the children in books but also to ensure, to the extent possible, that the reading habit continued when they went back to their hostels after the classes were over. 'We have residential facilities here,' he said, 'and I would like them to continue their relationship with books after games and the day's homework is done.'

I looked around the Chris Bake Library with its collection of 'good reads' and gems of literature. Books could indeed weave their magic on young minds, and I thought I would go a step further and work out a methodology whereby children could recall and remember the books they had read. And what better setting for my programme than the library? I told the principal I preferred to speak to the teachers, who would then act as catalysts and inspire the children. I asked if teachers from Class 4 onwards could be spared for an hour and a half to begin with. Later, I would speak to the teachers of the primary school with very young children.

I began by requesting the teachers to help me rearrange the tables and chairs in a round-table setting so that I would be talking 'with' them and not 'to' them. I also requested for the librarian to be present. If children were to use the library more, it had to be a more friendly place and a hub of activity, I said. So, could we download and put up attractive wall-charts giving more information on authors and books and involve the children in this? If the children were involved in library activity, a sense of 'belonging' could be created. The same could be done by allowing children to access books freely in the library and in case a page or a cover got torn accidentally, they could be given paper, glue and scissors and asked to 'repair' the book. This was what I had told teachers in my interactions with them in many other schools across the country. A child who has repaired a book is not likely to tear another again. We also needed to have storytelling sessions and activities around stories from suitable books in the library. Such activities would make children more familiar with the library and make the space more lively too. We needed to observe silence when reading or consulting books, of course, but there were other times when some 'noise' could be tolerated.

I said the CBSE in its wisdom had recently 'prescribed'

some classics for supplementary and general reading, but we could not get the children to read merely by thrusting books into their hands. The books had to be made interesting. In other words, they had to come alive in the hands of the children. I showed the teachers a library resource book I carried, *Classic Connections—How to hook the children on to reading the classics?* The book advocated the use of both audio and visual supports to help in reading. The school could invest in both audio books and film versions of the classics that had been prescribed by CBSE.

Taking *The Count of Monte Cristo* by Alexandre Dumas off a shelf, I asked the teachers if they knew the book had an Indian connection. Intrigued, they asked me to elaborate. I had enjoyed telling the story many times before, and launched into it again. When Edmund Dantes is betrayed and incarcerated in the prison Chateau d'If, he befriends an old monk, the abbé Faria, who is in an adjoining cell. The monk dies but not before telling Dantes about the treasure buried on the island of Monte Cristo. Dantes escapes by hiding in the burial shroud meant for the monk and eventually makes his way to the island. He discovers the treasure and sets himself up as the 'Count of Monte Cristo' and takes revenge on his betrayers. That was the plot, but did the teachers know that Abbe Faria was a real person and lived in Goa over three hundred years ago? He left Goa for Portugal and from there went on to Europe for further study. He was the father of hypnotism and had studied it as a science and had even written the first of a projected four-volume study, *The Origins of Lucid Sleep*. There was even a rumour that Faria had met Antoine Mesmer (the father of mesmerism) and had got the better of him in a hypnotic duel! Dumas had met Faria when he was imprisoned in the Bastille in Paris and had been so impressed that he had modelled his fictional Faria on him. As a finale, I asked the teachers how many of them had been to Goa on a holiday and visited Panjim, the capital. A few hands went up. I told them, that if they ever organized an excursion trip for the children to Goa—and I hoped they did—they should show the children the statue of Abbe Faria in Panjim; he is shown gesturing to a woman in a hypnotic trance. The sight wouldn't fail to intrigue and fascinate the children. They would remember it for long, and they would remember Dumas's classic. But before that, the book needed to be read and discussed!

To demonstrate the dramatic effort of storytelling, I picked up a copy of *The Oxford Book of Humorous Prose*, edited by Frank Muir, also in the library. I resolved to read a short story by the American humorist James Thurber, 'The Unicorn in the Garden'. The story, written in the 1930s when Thurber was a staffer with the *New Yorker*, remains a classic even today, though Thurber is better known for *The Secret Life of Walter Mitty*, which had an early film version, starring the inimitable Walter Matthau, and a more modern version with Ben Stiller in it. I knew the story by heart but read from the book to demonstrate how reading can be made interesting. I enjoyed reading out this story of how a husband gets the better of his wife to an audience consisting almost entirely of women teachers! (Male teachers seem to be an endangered species, and this was true at the Kings School too.)

Having introduced an element of humour—and woken up any teachers I might have bored so much that they had dozed off!—I said a good book would always leave a distinct and profound impression on the reader if it was read fully and with some attention. But all readers, children and adults, had notoriously short attention spans these days. We often read a book only to get to the ending, and having done so, we tended to forget it all too soon. So how could our children be made to remember and recall memorable books they had read? I relied on Louise Colligan's support book published by Scholastic, *Help, I Have to Write a Book Report!* Colligan stressed that the book report was like an 'aide-memoire' and was quite different to a review. It consisted only of four paragraphs. I looked through Colligan's prescription and amended it slightly while retaining its basic structure. I now asked the teachers if the children could do a small reader's report, after reading the book, in exactly four paragraphs. The first para would be a summary of the book. The second para would mention the author's main idea, the setting, the main action described, and the subject classification of the book. The third para would be about one of the main characters described in the book whom the reader had liked or disliked. (Colligan had subsumed this under the second para, and had not mentioned 'negative' characters at all. But I felt if an author could portray negativity in a character effectively, the job had been done well, and we do remember negative characters quite well, sometimes more than the others.) The fourth para of the report would be a conclusion giving the reader's opinion of the book.

I was rather pleased with myself when the principal told me he loved the idea! Soon after, I learned that a 'Reader's Report' sheet was stapled to the back of most books in the Chris Bake Library, to be filled by children who borrowed the books. When books were returned, the reports were discussed in class separately. They helped children to remember books they had read and recommend them to their friends.

ALEXANDRIA—A LIBRARY FOR THE SENSES

We were in Bengaluru to visit our friends Usha and Ram. Usha had just published her novel, *The Escapists of J. Mullick Road*, and the family, on move from Kolkata, had shifted into their spanking new house just off the old airport road. There was a double reason to celebrate, as the house had been quite some years in the making, for Usha is a fastidious architect, very particular about design. Usha was keen to know what my wife, also an architect, would make of it. Usha had used concrete very creatively in her design, which impressed my wife, and for my part, I was happy to see that Usha had at last managed to display her large collection of books. Shelves soared up to the ceiling from the floor, all stacked with books.

Usha's house was located in an upmarket, gated residential colony called Epsilon, and I wondered if all the residents in the complex knew the historical connotations of the term. Today, the term Epsilon has a variety of meanings in the physical and computer sciences and in economics and astronomy. It is also the name of one of the bigger data gathering and analysis companies. More popularly known as the fifth letter of the Greek alphabet, Epsilon has an interesting historical connotation. It was one of the five sections of the ancient city of Alexandria founded by Alexander the Great. The others were Alpha, Beta, Gamma and Delta.

Alexander came to Egypt in 332 BC. At an isthmus washed by the twin waters of the sea and Lake Mareotis, he found a location favourable to the founding of a city. Plutarch, the great Greek historian, who was to write a fine biography of the young Greek king, tells us that Alexander himself sketched the city's grid lines. There was not enough chalk at hand for Alexander to sketch the outlines of the city walls on the ground, but one of the builders in the team that accompanied Alexander had the bright idea of using flour from the rations of the king's soldiers to do the needful. All Greek soldiers in Alexander's army carried rations during their long marches and campaigns, so there was enough flour for the purpose. Thus, the grid lines of the proposed city were duly marked. But then, Plutarch goes on to tell us, a great variety of birds—pelicans, ibis, herons, owls, hoopoes and kingfishers—arose from Lake Mareotis, swooped down and ate up some of the flour on the ground. Alexander was apparently quite disturbed by this, but was reassured by his soothsayers that this was a good omen, for it signified that the new city would prosper in all things, especially in the fruits of the earth, and would be a great provider of food for a great many nations. Alexander then ordered the builders to proceed in the building of the great city.

But the obliteration of some of the grid lines was to have an effect on the layout of Alexandria. Today, we know that Beta was to the north and housed the palaces, the Museum with its Great Library, and Delta was to the east and contained the Jewish quarter. But the locations of the Alpha, Gamma and Epsilon sections are not known at all. Sadly, Alexander himself was never to see the city that would be named after him. He died in Babylon in 323 BC and his body was brought back to Alexandria by Ptolemy Soter and buried in a golden sarcophagus in a mausoleum worthy of Alexander's stature. But the sarcophagus was plundered for its gold later, and today, Alexander lies in a plain glass sarcophagus with a broken nose. It is stated that Octavian Caesar, later Emperor Augustus of Rome, wanted to see Alexander's body and in the process, also touched it and broke Alexander's nose. Thus, Alexander too has a broken house—ironically, after his death, having braved so many wars in his lifetime—very similar to that of the great Sphinx near the Pyramids of Gaza (the latter a deliberate disfigurement by the French soldiers of Napoleon).

But in one respect, the ancient omen foretold to Alexander so many years ago came to be true. Both Alexander and Egypt as a whole were to provide food and grain to a number of nations, including Rome in Julius Caesar's time and later. But the city of Alexandria itself became famous in history for providing another form of nourishment, that of learning and knowledge in the form of the Great Library of Alexandria. Today, this great library exists only in the imagination, having been destroyed completely by a fire. No painting or visual rendering of the library exists, just the fragment of an ancient scroll, that must once have been a priceless manuscript for scholars. It was Ptolemy Soter who built the library in memory of Alexander and established it as one of the greatest centres of learning in the ancient world, worthy of a great king. Today, what we have in the place of the ancient library is the Bibliotheca Alexandrina, situated very near the site of the original, and what a magnificent library it is!

I had been invited in the year 2006 to visit Bogota in Colombia which had been declared as a world book capital by UNESCO in 2007. Delhi too had been a previous world book capital in 2003 and the Bogota authorities had invited delegates from the previous world book capitals to share their experiences, so that Bogota could better plan its activities for 2007. At our meeting, Ronya Naim from the library director's office in Alexandria made a presentation on the new library, the Bibliotheca Alexandrina. Alexandria had been chosen as the first world book capital in 2001 as a fitting tribute to a city that had such a magnificent tradition of books, manuscripts, knowledge and learning. It was Ronya's wonderful presentation on the new library that opened our eyes to how fittingly this tradition had been continued by the Norwegian architectural firm of Snohetta and the new, bold and evocative design by architects Thorsen, Kapeller and Dykster. The design was chosen after an international competition and as Ronya took us through its many features—including how four storeys of the library had been constructed below sea level—my wife and I decided we must visit and see this marvel for ourselves. That opportunity was to come in 2010, when the family was to visit Egypt and we decided to drive down to Alexandria from Cairo. But before that, I had to know more about the legacy of the architects and what they had to live up to.

*

It is said the great library of Alexandria was a model of the library of Pisistratus in Athens, a great centre of Greek learning. But Ptolemy Soter wanted to make Alexandria even greater and attract scholars from all over the world. For that, he needed to get manuscripts, a great many of them, as part of the library collections. An order went out that every ship wanting to berth at the port of Alexandria had to part with its manuscripts in order for the library staff to make copies. The ships were warned that this would take time, for all manuscripts needed to be copied by hand. If a particular captain and his crew were in a hurry, the ship had to forfeit its manuscripts! There was not too much concern for copyright or intellectual property at the time, and Ptolemy's agents went all over the Mediterranean looking for manuscripts. In addition, Ptolemy wrote personal letters to all the sovereigns of the known world, asking them to lend their manuscripts and books for copying. Athens lent him the texts of Euripides, Sophocles and Aeschylus. It is speculated that it had been Alexander's wish that the first librarian should be a universally acknowledged figure of learning. Accordingly,

Ptolemy managed to recruit Demetrius of Phaleron as the first librarian. Demetrius had been a student of Aristotle and in his supervision, the library was meant to be much more than a mere depository of scrolls and manuscripts.

Under Demetrius, the library would welcome scholars from Greece and from other parts of the world to work side-by-side. Studies were pursued in mathematics and medicine, literature and poetry, physics and philosophy. The library was to be universal and it had a tall order, to collect everything that had been known to be written then. The library's collections grew over the years and it soon had 700,000 mixed papyrus scrolls with multiple works and another 90,000 single scrolls. The desire to possess or collect great works was so overpowering, that it is said Ptolemy kept back the original works of Euripides, Sophocles and Aeschylus, thus forfeiting the 15 talents he had deposited as a security bond!

Soon, additional scrolls were housed in another library, located nearby, the 'daughter' library—the Serapeion, housed in the temple of Serapis. Even Julius Caesar, chasing Pompey Magnus into Alexandria, was said to have consulted scrolls in the library. Some of the most important scholars in the history of learning have been associated with the library, some even as its librarians. Aristarchus was the first person to say the earth revolved around the sun. Eratosthenes, a past head librarian, proved the earth was spherical and calculated its circumference. Hipparchus developed the first atlas of the stars. Euclid wrote his *Elements of Geometry* in the Alexandria Library. Zenodutus and Alexandrian grammarians established the basis of literary scholarship. Archimedes was a visiting scholar. These scholars and the ones who came after them established Alexandria as the foremost centre of learning in the world.

But the library suffered a slow decline from the time of Julius Caesar, though later Cleopatra did try to do her best to revive it. There are different versions of how the great library was ravaged by fire and destroyed. It is now believed that it was not one fire but a series of fires, at different times, that finally wiped off the library. A part of the library was accidentally destroyed by Caesar's Alexandrian wars when he allied with Cleopatra against her half-brother Ptolemy, the boy king. Ptolemy had hoped to secure Caesar's alliance when he severed Pompey's head as a sign of friendship. It was with Caesar's help that Cleopatra secured the throne of Egypt. The alliance with Rome was to prove useful when Mark Antony donated 200,000 scrolls to Cleopatra for the Serapeion to compensate for the destruction of a part of the main great library. Subsequent wars between rival armies and fire from ships too could have triggered off fires in the library, since it was located in close proximity to the sea. We do have some evidence now that almost 40,000 manuscripts stored in the warehouses adjoining the harbour were destroyed by fire.

A later story, possibly apocryphal, for the dates don't quite match, speaks of the great library being sacked and burnt by invading Islamic armies. The story goes like this. When the Arab commander of the invading army in 641 AD found the great collection of scrolls in the library, he was faced with the predicament of what to do with them. He apparently managed to send word to the Caliph Omar, through what means is not clear, about the manuscripts and asking for instructions on their disposal. The instructions from the Great Caliph were simple and direct: If the content of the manuscripts were in accordance with the Holy Book, then there was no real need to keep them, for the Holy book sufficed. If, on the other hand, the content differed from that of the Holy Book, they needed to be destroyed, for they were against the true faith. It isn't known what means were employed by the commander to 'read' the numerous manuscripts—if the stories are true, which they appear not to be, he probably did not bother overmuch with this nicety, for the common thread running through both sets of instructions was clear: 'Destroy the scrolls.' This, apparently, was duly done, but the stock of scrolls was so great that the fires burned continuously for some months, much like the fires that are believed to have destroyed the invaluable manuscripts in the libraries of Nalanda and elsewhere, later. It is also said that some of the manuscripts fed the fires that warmed the public baths established in Alexandria.

I had read all this history, and also remembered Ronya's presentation on the new library in Bogota, when we went to Alexandria from Cairo in 2010. We were returning the same day and I was conscious that we had to take in a lot with the limited time at our disposal. My wife, being an architect, was excited to see Snohetta's design, for the firm had won the design competition against some very reputed firms. Snohetta too must have been conscious of the Alexandrian legacy and their architectural brief must have had quite a bit of history, apart from the client's requirements. There was really no way to get away from the history, for the site chosen for the new library was almost identical to the area where the great library once stood. My wife and I were both curious to see how Snohetta had managed it. Nothing quite prepared us for what we saw. The new library was designed as a simple circle, 160 metres in diameter. It went from 15.8 metres below ground—with some of it below sea level—to 37 metres above ground. Seen from above, it approximated the image of the sun, a homage to the Egyptian sun god Ra, represented in hieroglyphics as a circular disk. The roof, we saw, was slanting, partly glazed, and the slant was in such a manner that it attracted sunlight throughout the year. To access the library, we had to cross a moat, which serves as a border.

As you enter the library, you see a viewing platform called the Callimachus Triangle. Callimachus was a Greek poet from Cyrene. He was probably one of the assistants to Zenodutus in the library, and in time, became a librarian of Alexandria but internal politics and rivalries prevented his becoming the head librarian. Yet, the architects of Snohetta along with the present-day administrators of the library had chosen him as a pivotal figure in the new library. For it was Callimachus who had painstakingly catalogued all the great library's holdings by subject and by author, with a short description of each work. He composed the *Pinakes*, now a lost bibliographic work and perhaps the first catalogue of the great library of Alexandria. All subsequent librarians had to be grateful to Callimachus for the system of referencing and cataloguing which made their work so much easier. With Callimachus began the discipline of library science, and he fully deserved the position of head librarian. Posterity was now trying to right this wrong. From the Callimachus Triangle, it was not difficult to witness the poet at work, looking down at the floor which supports the exterior curving wall, 180 metres wide, and 80-metre-deep space terraces at ten levels with viewing platforms on each giving an unrestricted view in every direction.

The Callimachus Triangle

Book stacks extended behind each terrace and could be accessed independently through an external platform. The library gently slopes to the left and has been designed in such a way that the last four floors are below sea level. Solar shades installed on the ceiling allow diffused sunlight into the library. Recessed lighting and the skylights allow plenty of light. The skylights symbolize eyes and the solar shades, eyelashes. The book stacks are lit by individual lights on the racks. To maintain a historical continuum, the side panellings have built-in recesses, as if they were storing scrolls. Books are arranged by subject, beginning with the roots of knowledge, like philosophy, history, mathematics and religion, and ending with digital technology.

In spite of the constant flow of visitors, silence is maintained so that working scholars are not disturbed, and working tables and the stacks are placed away from the main visitor areas. Each working table had a computer table but it was gratifying to see students reading and making notes from books diligently. Clearly, all the world's knowledge was not on the internet as yet. In keeping with what the great Alexander had wished and what Ptolemy Soter implemented at the great library, the new library at Alexandria has become a centre for the production and dissemination of knowledge and a place of dialogue and understanding between people of diverse faiths, cultures and regions.

We gathered that the general section of the library holds about 500,000 books and about 25,000 journals, along with an internet centre and archives. Among the most distinguishing features of the library are its specialized units—for the arts, multimedia and audio-visual projects, specialized material for the visually impaired, and reading material for children and young adults. There is a microfilm unit along with a rare books and special collections section. The precious fragment of that ancient scroll, a living reminder of the library's ancient legacy, is housed in a special enclosure under a glass case. In keeping with this legacy, the library also houses three museums: for antiquities, manuscripts and the history of science. It also has a planetarium, a concert hall, a conference centre and four art galleries. Among the permanent exhibits, impressions of Alexandria, Arab calligraphy, the history of writing and instruments of history and science are part of the regular itinerary of visitors. Among the specialized activities are two projects. One, to introduce young people to the hybrid world of the electronic and the printed word and take this to schools through a specially designed book-mobile; the second, to provide training to budding librarians, of which Callimachus would have approved.

A walk on the promenade outside the library is enriching. The blue water of the moat from a distance seems to merge with the blue of the Mediterranean and gives an impression that the library is floating on water. An indicator, perhaps, that a library has the ability to travel and bring knowledge and learning to people in different lands. The plaza outside has a bust of Alexander to remind everyone as to who had inspired the great library. Our guide was eager to show us one of the latest acquisitions of the library, a 'book express machine' that can print and deliver a book—'in all of fifteen minutes' the guide told us proudly! What he overlooked was the full-sized statue of Demetrius of Phaleron, the founding father of the great library of Alexandria. Fittingly, perhaps, Demetrius had his back turned to the book express machine!

A prominent and notable feature on the exterior wall is a giant slab of granite quarried from the mines at Aswan. It has a word from the languages and civilizations of the world showing that the library at Alexandria stood for a plurality of cultures and access to knowledge for all. We looked hard for a word from one of the Indian languages. We spotted it at last. My wife was able to read the language. It was the Malayalam word 'nee', which means 'you' and also has the same meaning in Tamil.

On the drive back to Cairo, I pondered on the significance of this one word from an Indian language among the many that adorned the wall of the new library in Alexandria. Though the word may have been picked at random, I thought it had a significance. Inscribing the word 'you', those who conceived the new library seemed to indicate that its future would depend on 'us', a collective of 'you'. At a time when overt imperial conquests which destroyed libraries are at an end, we still hear of libraries being closed down in different parts of the world. This can only be prevented if 'we' take collective action and become stakeholders in the continuance of libraries for the welfare of the community as a whole—and a community that is not singular and exclusive, but plural and inclusive.

CITIES OF WORDS

This is a tribute to two 'library cities' I have been fortunate to visit over the years, and in both I saw what dedicated book places like libraries can do if they become an intrinsic, integral and, if I may add, indispensable part of the community they serve. Geographically, the two places could not be further apart on the global map, but in a fundamental way they are the closest of neighbours. The first is located in Japan and the other in Colombia.

Under the auspices of the Japan Foundation, I had been selected to join a group of publishers from diverse countries—Thailand, Malaysia, Indonesia and Australia, apart from India. There were two delegates from each country and my fellow countryman was Dilip Padhi, an Odia publisher from Sambalpur. The itinerary was carefully put together by the Japan Foundation in Tokyo to ensure we were given as much of a literary exposure as possible. Security considerations were also paramount, as the trip took place just after the 9/11 incidents in the US in 2001. I was working with OUP India at the time and there had been a worldwide advisory from our Oxford office asking managers not to travel abroad from their home base in the wake of 9/11. Fortunately, our travel dates were in November of that year, just after the travel advisory was lifted. It was a two-week trip and after landing in Tokyo, I was happy to find that the hosts had organized trips to Hiroshima, Osaka and Kyoto too. The Foundation had obviously taken some help from publishers to put together our itinerary, and while part of the reason was to see if we could initiate some collaborative projects, the primary aim was, I suspect, to show all of us that the print book was alive and flourishing in Japan, along with a vibrant reading culture.

It is important to emphasize this, as everywhere we went, we saw young people on their phones accessing and playing games. The reading seemed to consist of the 'manga', a book in graphic form, and 'bunko', a short book in B format. The emphasis was on reading matter that could be finished quickly. The manga dominated the books market. I distinctly remember our visit to a major distributor with a bewildering degree of computerization and robotic technology whose business was entirely that of manga. Normal print books, it seemed, were nowhere in evidence.

To dispel this impression and to change our perception, our hosts along with our interpreter and guide, Eiko Sato, had organized a day trip to the Uruyasu Public Library about an hour-and-a-half run by bus from our hotel in Shinjuku. Urayasu is a small town in the Chiba Prefecture, very close to Disneyland, Japan's marvel and joy. It has a population of 130,000 and right from the start, we could see that the library occupied a central space in people's lives. The director of the library, Tokoyoda-san, greeted us warmly, and in his presentation, showed us how with zeal, enthusiasm and dedication, a model institution could be created to serve the needs of the community. There were seven libraries in the city, of which the Uruyasu Public Library in Chiba was the biggest. The library was closely integrated with the lives of the people, most of whom were only a ten-minute walk away. The popularity of the library could be gauged from the fact that on an average, twelve-to-thirteen books were borrowed per person, per year.

Japan publishes about 70,000 books in hardcover every year and the library purchased half the number annually on a budget of 140 million yen. The director told us proudly that the number of books borrowed had doubled over the last twenty years and we could see the reason why. The reading rooms were full of people from the community, either absorbed in their reading or busy researching some valuable reference material. But it was the spacious section dedicated to children that drew our attention. Adolescents and young children were either getting books issued or were reading at the table. We were delightedly astonished to see three- to four-year-old toddlers being brought in by the hand by their mothers who then read aloud to them. The children were listening intently and in rapt attention. So as not to disturb them, I quietly went over to a rack where there were a number of folk and fairy tales in Japanese. I was happy to see a number of translations from Indian tales too! I was confident that an interest in stories and books at this young age would make the children turn into serious readers when they attained adolescence and adulthood.

To ensure that children who could not come to the Uruyasu Library were not deprived of the hours of pleasure storytelling can bring, the library had a very active outreach programme. It had started storytelling programmes in schools about famous characters who were already familiar to the children. The storytelling sessions were combined with story-reading sessions from books, so that the children would form a relationship with the physical book. The children related more to attractive picture books at this stage and the library staff always ensured they had an adequate stock of these. It was a thrill for the children to see pictures of their favourite characters. These programmes were conducted about 700 times in the course of a year, and at the director's initiative, and because some of the children were very young and a little fearful and hesitant, mothers too were encouraged to join the children. Small children of the ages one to four were paired with their mothers and encouraged to sing songs and rhymes. For older children, even a bit of play-acting was encouraged. The children were reassured by the presence of a parent and slowly began to overcome their initial hesitation and apprehension.

The library also had outreach services for members who were physically and visually challenged. Library staff visited them about 400 times a year and attended to their requirements. The visually challenged received updated manuals for their specially designed computers so that they could read independently. In addition, the staff ensured that the latest books of their choice were also uploaded on to their systems. A mobile library service also regularly made rounds of hospitals and nursing homes so that the sick and injured did not lack books for reading. The library staff had special reading sessions for those who were too weak to make the effort. The director, Tokoyoda-san, was convinced that the reading sessions were therapeutic and had as much to do with the patients' recovery as the medicines they were given!

I pondered over all this during the ride back to our hotel, the Keio Plaza in Shinjuku. It had indeed been a very pleasurable visit, and one that had filled us all with hope and new energy. Publishing and bookselling aren't the easiest of professions, the challenges are great and numerous, but we had seen at close quarters how much value they added to human experience. At a formal reception by the Japan Foundation in our honour where the ambassadors of the countries of the visiting delegation were also present, I was invited to make the return speech on behalf of the delegation. In the presence of the then Indian ambassador, Aftab Seth, I referred to the salient features of our visit and was happy that print books were flourishing (e-books had yet to make an appearance in India). I particularly referred to the great work being done by the Uruyasu Public Library, no doubt emulated by other libraries, in keeping the reading culture alive in the country. I mentioned that Tokoyoda-san had, with a twinkle in his eye, extolled the virtues of Tokyo Disneyland, which was also in the Chiba Prefecture, and very near to us. He mentioned its tempting new features, including a Sea World. Thinking that he was referring to Disneyland as a bigger and better draw for children than a library or bookshop, we had nodded our heads in agreement. But Tokoyoda-san's intention was something more. The then annual budget for the Uruyasu library was 140 million yen, which roughly worked out to a little more than 1,000 yen per inhabitant of Uruyasu. The city government sanctioned the funds and part of its revenues came from the visitors' fees at Disneyland! 'The more the visitors there, the higher the revenues for the city and, possibly, more funds allocation for the library,' Tokoyoda-san had said, looking at us speculatively. But sadly, the Japan Foundation had not factored this in, I said, and there was no visit to Tokyo Disneyland on this trip for us!

*

The second such experience I had was in Bogota, Colombia. I travelled there in In 2007. UNESCO selects one city as the 'world book capital' every year, and in 2007, it was Bogota. The Bogota authorities, taking the task enjoined on them rather seriously, decided that they would invite delegates from the prvious world book capitals to make presentations on the programmes in their respective cities. The visit of the delegates was also scheduled to coincide with the annual book fair in Bogota as the director of programmes at Bogota world book capital, Ms Andrea Mejia Hernandez, was also the director of the book fair.

I was chosen as the delegate from Delhi somewhat curiously. Andrea had asked the former Colombian Ambassador to India, Ms Betancour, to suggest a publisher-delegate from Delhi. Betancour, in turn, contacted her close friend, M. Varadarajan (Varad) whom she had known as the Secretary, Department of Culture, Government of India, during her time in New Delhi. Varad, who was actually better known to my sister, Jaya, contacted me. I wasn't going to let the opportunity pass, and so it was that I received a letter of invitation from Andrea. My wife too decided to accompany me.

We were conscious during our trip that Bogota had acquired a name in the international press for all the wrong reasons. It had been labelled a drug country and had one of the largest illegal border trades in cocaine. The drug overlord Pablo Escobar was the boss of the Medellin drug cartel and in time the wealth he had amassed had made him the seventh richest man in the world. He had recently been eliminated by a joint force of US and Colombian authorities and his cartel broken up. But that was not the end of Colombia's problems. The country was riven with conflicts between the forces of the far left and the far right and murders and kidnappings were quite common. Along with all this, and quite paradoxically too, the country had a flourishing book culture, a network of libraries and strong reading habits, and this was what we had come to see.

In fact, it was a presentation on innovative programmes to promote reading in Bogota that had led to the city being chosen as the world book capital, and Andrea was determined to highlight this for us, and as we were, in a sense, informal ambassadors, we could be expected to carry back this image with us. Arriving in Bogota by a late evening flight from New York, we were grateful to be received at the airport and taken straight to the Hotel Tequendama, the leading hotel in Bogota. We were equally grateful to find ourselves in a suite, thoughtfully provided by Andrea. My wife was suitably impressed but I think it had more to do with her. As we were a couple, Andrea had thought we would be more comfortable in a suite in the famed hotel. But I remembered, a little uncomfortably, that the hotel had been used as a meeting centre by the Medellin drug cartel whenever they were in the city. Escobar's family had stayed in Tequendama before leaving the country. Well, he, at least, was no longer around.

The next day, our presentations on our experiences during our respective world book capital years were well received. Andrea had thoughtfully invited the envoys of the delegate countries and our ambassador at the time was Nilima Mitra whom I had met earlier during her tenure at the Foreign Services Institute (FSI) in Delhi. Andrea had been quite impressed with some of the programmes for increased reading that had been initiated in India, particularly those for children and young adults. At the end of my presentation, I mentioned that it was important for us to get symbols like sports-persons and celebrities to endorse reading. Could we get football stars, or the Formula One race driver Pablo Montoya, or even a diva like Shakira to endorse reading? It evoked many laughs but I was serious. I explained, 'Stars endorse all kinds of products except books; why we can't we rope them in to do this?' Children would certainly be motivated if they could see their idols up there with books and endorsing reading. The closest we had come in India was our cricket star Kapil Dev endorsing an English-speaking guide on television many years ago. Andrea agreed with me, except that she felt Shakira didn't particularly care for books!

Bogota had six very popular libraries (the number may be higher now), and we were fortunate that the organizers had arranged visits to two of the most remarkable of these. Along with the libraries, we were also lucky to visit the Botero museum dedicated to Fernando Botero, Colombia's leading artist. We also visited Simon Bolivar's house, which had also been converted into a museum, and here I was to reflect on Gabriel Garcia Marquez's book on the great Liberator, *The General in His Labyrinth*.

The first library that we visited was the Luis Angel Arrango Library, one of Bogota's best. It had some of the finest holdings on the history of Colombia and its art. The director, who had attended our presentation, was very dedicated to her task. She was proud to display a pronounced India connection and to show us the large number of curios and art pieces from India that decorated her office. I was surprised to see a large number of objects from the state of Kerala. 'Oh, I love Kerala,' she said, 'and I try to visit as often as possible.' She was happy to hear that both my wife and I had a Kerala connection, my wife having been born there. We had a fascinating discussion on the various art forms and dances of Kerala and its backwaters and scenic beauty. I spoke of its strong literary traditions and mentioned the role of the Sahitya Parishad in promoting the literary culture there. I said many of the authors in Malayalam had a strong readership, both in the state and in the larger diaspora settled outside the state. Some of them had achieved iconic status and were now being translated into English and other languages so that other people too could enjoy their writing. She spoke about how popular her library had become in the lives of the community and how the number of members had been growing steadily. She encouraged authors to have reading sessions and book discussions with the members of the public. This way, authors could get direct feedback from their readers—after all, she said, what were authors without a readership.

She was particularly interested in the programmes I did in schools back in India to strengthen reading and the role of the school library in getting children to both know books and their authors better. I told her about our experiments with the 'book report' forms and how this helped children recall easily the salient features of the books they read. She made extensive notes during our discussion and was interested in the DEAR programme that a few schools in India had adopted. It was an acronym and stood for 'Drop Everything and Read!' For the duration of a class period, once or twice in a term, the whole school dropped whatever they were doing, picked up a book and read. All staff, including the principal and support staff, teachers and children, read. It had to be a general book that would be relevant to all. In the morning assembly, a student from each class would be selected to narrate the learning from the book and demonstrate its relevance. Slowly, a reading culture—

reading for pleasure, and mindful reading, above all—would develop. The director listened intently to all this. She had a magnificent, illustrated book on Colombian art on her desk. We had been idly leafing through the book and seeing the pictures. Sensing our interest, she said she would like to make a gift, and in the evening, a copy of the rather expensive book was sent to our hotel room!

But the best was yet to come.

Can we ever imagine that rubbish, garbage or general waste, can have anything to do with books or reading? The reader may be forgiven for thinking I am proposing an alchemy whereby rubbish can be converted into print matter or books. The nearest we have come to this is a process whereby waste of a certain kind can be converted to coarse paper. But we were to see this relationship in a strikingly new light on our next visit in Bogota. We were driven to a library almost on the outskirts of the town. On the way, my wife was excited to see a part of the city that had been designed by the famous French architect Le Corbusier, who had also designed the Indian city of Chandigarh. She knew that Corbusier had worked in Bogota but had not planned to see his work. Anyway, we happened to drive past on our way to a library that, according to our hosts, was 'different'; they hadn't told us exactly how. Soon, we came to a less privileged section of the city and passing through a gate, drove up to a building. The bus stopped near the building and as we alighted, my wife took a look and felt, surely this could not be a library, as it flouted every design sense. There were a number of young people milling around and the explanation came from the young director of the library who came across to meet us. He spoke in Spanish and Paulina Jaramillo translated for us. The director said that the building had been designed not as a library but as the city's rubbish dump! The driveway through which we had come was the same that was once used by dumpsters to unload rubbish. There were incinerators installed inside the building to burn the waste and three giant chimneys to expel the smoke. He said a few years ago the city's rubbish dump had shifted, possibly they needed a new, bigger place as the city had grown. There was a debate in the city council about what to do with the existing building. Various proposals had been made—convert it into a mall, a theatre, a nursing home or even a school. But one sane voice, the councillor from the local area, suggested, 'Why not have a library, particularly for children and young adults?' There was no such library available for young people in the neighbourhood and children had to travel quite some distance to access books. They were losing interest in books, the councillor had said, and it was very likely that they might stop reading altogether.

His views gathered support in the council and a major decision was made to convert the building into a public library, but mainly for adolescents and children. 'What you now see before you,' said the director proudly, 'is the Biblioteca Publica El Tintal Manuel Zapata Olivella.' The building had been converted into a library by a truly innovative design by the Colombian architect Daniel Bermudez, who had been cited internationally for his work. The library was opened in 2001 and had been named after Manual Zapata Olivelle, who had been an anthropologist, a doctor and a writer. He had been born in the Cordoba area of Bogota. The director told us that some of his works had been translated into English and published in the United States.

Biblioteca Publica El Tintal

We had already seen young people in animated conversation outside the building, and now the director took us inside. It was fairly buzzing with activity. Young adults were getting books issued, some were in rooms, reading, and others were taking notes. There were story-reading and storytelling sessions going on in different rooms. The library even had a toddlers' playtime and activities room; perhaps the library doubled up as a part-time crèche. 'We encourage authors of children's books and even book illustrators to come and talk to our children,' said the director. I knew that when authors spoke about their work, it helped readers understand their work better. If an illustrator could be persuaded to demonstrate, the children would relate much more closely to the book. The director also said that they had special screening rooms where they showed the young people movies based on the books they had read or discussed. The movie sessions were organized only after the children had read the print version of the book. 'We want them to form their own mental images of the main characters in the book, before seeing the movie.' They had screened movie versions of many of the world's classics and they were proving to be very popular. I noticed that one such movie session was about to start, and small children had formed an orderly queue outside the room.

There was another positive outcome of the establishment of the library. The director told us that in the five years that the library had been in existence, there had been hardly any reports of petty thefts or small crimes in the area, as the children were now otherwise occupied. We were happy, because we had heard that cases of children being lured into a life of vice and crime, of being used as 'drug mules' by gangs that seemed to operate freely, were all too common in Bogota.

In later years, we would hear the story of yet another connection between rubbish and books. Jose Alberto Gutierrez, a rubbish collector, found Tolstoy's classic *Anna Karenina* in the rubbish one day and that changed his life. Books became a fascination and he was to go on to collect 25,000 books over a period of seventeen years. He was appalled that people in affluent neighbourhoods threw great books in the garbage, when there were thousands who could benefit from reading the books but had no money to buy them, or even access to libraries. He has today converted his modest home in his neighbourhood into a library of 'rescued' books and runs a free library for children. Now that space has run out in his home, he takes books around in a van and donates them to less privileged people in and around Bogota. He believes that education, access to books and reading can break the cycle of poverty. He has become a celebrity in Bogota now with an endless stream of children visiting his house every day. They call him 'the lord of books'.

And then there's the story of the amazing Luis Soriano, who carries a mobile library on two donkeys to homes in rural and remote parts of Colombia. He had been doing this for twenty years when we heard of him on that trip to Bogota. His faithful donkeys were appropriately named 'Alfa' and 'Beto', recalling the letters of the Greek alphabet and the first two sections, 'Alpha' and 'Beta', of the fabled and ancient city of Alexandria, home to the ancient world's greatest library. Yet, Soriano was modest about his achievements. Out of 1,000 children who accessed his books, he said, only fifty made some realistic use of them. But for the fifty, their lives would be changed forever!

Andrea Mejia Hernandez had been brilliantly successful in changing the international perception about Bogota during that world book capital year of 2007. She was to later become a minister in the Colombian government and, hopefully, was able to carry the good work.